D0609332

HOME BUSINESS STARTUP BIBLE
by RENAE CHRISTINE

Rich Mom™

HOME BUSINESS STARTUP BIBLE

by RENAE CHRISTINE

Copyright © 2013 by Renae Christine

ALL RIGHTS RESERVED. No part of this book may be reproduced or transmitted in any form by any means, electronic or mechanical, including photocopying and recording, or by any information storage and retrieval system, except as may be expressly permitted in writing from the publisher except by a reviewer who may quote brief passages in critical articles or reviews. Requests for permission should be addressed to by Renae Christine, ATTN: Renae Christine, 6935 Aliante Pkwy. Ste. #104-273, Las Vegas, NV 89084.

This book's purpose is to provide accurate and authoritative information on the topics covered. It is sold with the understanding that neither the author nor the publisher is engaged in rendering legal, financial, accounting and other professional services. The advice contained herein may not be suitable for your situation. Please consult with a professional where appropriate. The author and publisher shall not be liable for any loss of profit or commercial damages.

Editors: Daniel Magill and Martin Coffee
Interior Design: Akasha Archer
Cover Design: Renae Christine

ISBN 978-1-62620-425-6

Printed in the United States of America

10 9 8 7 6 5 4 3 2 1

Dedicated to my Besties

Contents

Preface

I have written this book for you, the reader, out of a passionate anger-love rage.

I know I'm not supposed to say that, but it's true.

My husband was a musician without any steady work and I was the breadwinner of the family when I left my position as editor-in-chief of a local weekly Las Vegas newspaper so I could be a stay-at-home mom.

Most of my friends and family wondered how our little family would survive. Many who knew us made wagers on the amount of time it would take for us to come to our senses and for either my husband or myself to get "a real job."

After five years of both my husband and I working from home, some of those same family members and friends came to me asking how I did it and how they could do the same.

Eventually, I simply ran out of time to help everyone I loved—and I love everyone. I searched online for a work-at-home resource so that my friends and family could do what I was doing without me having to continue working 16 hours a day to help each one personally.

This is where my passionate anger-love rage comes in.

It seems that every book out there for stay-at-home moms trying to start a business is either a mommy millionaire book that is way out of reach for most moms or mommy business books which contain chapters such as:

Living With Less
Frugal Living
Family Budgets

Are you kidding me? How utterly depressing. This is not the advice moms need to start a business.

This book is different.

This book is for all you stay-at-home moms that desire the same pay as your working husbands and the same respect as a brick-and-mortar business and still stay at home with your kids.

This book is for moms low on cash but high on hopes and dreams. It's for the moms who have both good days and bad with their kids, who strive for perfection but know they'll never reach it.

This book is the starting point.

I'll teach you everything you need to know to get your home business going. If you've already started your business, then this book may not be for you. This book will cover every single basic step to get your business set up and moving smoothly. After that, you can come to me to help you expand that business and that's when the fun truly begins.

Until then, starting a business can be grueling work and it can take an entire year just to get an amazing start-up business roaring.

This time frame may seem daunting, but if you take a look at any worthwhile task—like potty training for example—you know it can take a while and requires patience, but eventually, it's worth more than what you put into it.

Many online business book authors do a disservice to their readers by saying that anyone can start a business that runs itself in a week or less and the money is automated and comes rolling in without any work. Those authors are trying to sell you something and shouldn't be trusted.

Many of those same authors have never had an online business selling something besides their own "how to start a business" products, so they have little or no experience in the industry in the first place. My first businesses were in the stationery industry.

I have never had to pay a dime for advertising for those businesses since 2006 when they began and they are still going strong with two assistants to help me run it while I make funny YouTube videos to help work-at-home moms (http://richmombusiness.com) and write this book for you. Shout out to my assistants! I love you!

I've also found that other work-at-home books tend to be like text books, filled with options, but no opinions on which option is most popular or best. Since I've built so many businesses myself, I have very strong opinions on the very best tools and options to use.

I'll be listing my favorite sites, resources and tools here with not a single sales link. I am not being paid in any way for the tools and sites I list in this book nor am I an affiliate of any of them. I simply love them for solving my own problems as a business owner and hope they can solve your problems in the same way.

You might have a different opinion or resource in mind while reading this book, but I hope you'll find one or two of my resource nuggets useful that you wouldn't have found otherwise.

Foreword

One day, not long ago, someone commented on my blog, "You're Awesome-Sauce, Allie!"

When someone refers to you as "awesome sauce" with a big smile, well, one becomes intrigued. I mean, who uses a phrase like "awesome sauce"? Is she crazy or just excited to be working from home? I had to discover who this person was.

That person was Renae Christine.

I am a WAHM. No, it is not a secret group that you join to do mysterious activities. It simply refers to a "work at home mom"; a mom who has decided to run a business from her home. Work at home moms operate many different types of businesses. I've chosen to work online as a blogger and social media marketer. I specialize in helping other work at home moms expand their business presence online. And so does Renae.

If you have watched any of Renae's videos you quickly realize how charismatic she is. She uses her own made up terms like "awesome sauce" and "besties". That is who Renae is, one who paves her own way and creates new paths. She has started and run many businesses and wears many coats. I am proud to know her as a friend and a colleague.

Home Business Startup Bible is compiled from Renae's own knowledge. A book of instructions she has forged from years of experience- failures and successes. You get a peek into how Renae has reached a place where she can say her family is closer due to the fact she works from home. And accomplish this for yourself. Renae makes you feel you are her "bestie", a term she warmly uses to refer to her readers and fellow business women online. She may seem a little crazy but she is also excited and passionate to be doing what she does. As you start your own business, receiving advice from an entrepreneur who is excited about her job to help you is a blessing. Reading and implementing the information in Home Business Startup Bible you will become "awesome sauce" too.

~Allie
Ramblings of a WAHM http://www.ramblingsofawahm.com

Introduction

Before I graduated college, I was offered the editor-in-chief position at a Las Vegas weekly newspaper. So what did I do? I took it . . . for one week. Then I quit to be a stay-at-home mom.

So what's next? I thought. Did I really just get a BA degree in journalism and turn down a huge opportunity to sit here and change poopy diapers?

I thought of creating a business, and though I heard a startling statistic that 9 out of 10 businesses fail, I ventured forward anyway, thinking that if everything blew up in my face I would simply just have to do it 9 more times before one of the businesses would stick and succeed.

In full disclosure, a few of my first businesses blew up in my face rather horrifically –it wasn't pretty. Eventually though, through my failures, I learned more through each business and worked out a formula to create successful businesses.

The first action I took when I discovered the formula for success was to see if I could duplicate it. Once I had succeeded again and again, I felt confident enough to automate the process. And now I'm ready to share all of that hard-earned knowledge and experience with you.

These days, I take my kids to visit museums, go to the movies, Chuck E. Cheeses (I hate that place) and get involved in all kinds of exciting activities, without having to worry about sticking to a strict budget.

No, we are not millionaires. But I no longer study the tags at the grocery store to see which bag of cheerios is really cheaper per ounce.

I no longer get a lump in my throat when we have car trouble and I'm scared we don't have enough in savings to fix the problem. In fact, now we hardly ever have car trouble (knock on wood) because we have a decent set of cars that we own outright.

There is something to be said for living comfortably for a change and being able to take your kids to Disneyland without cringing at the cost.

My family has grown closer together because my husband and I are both able to work from home with our kids coloring next to us and we are happier than we have been at any other time in our lives.

Can money buy you happiness?

In all truthfulness, yes, I believe it can.

Follow me through these pages. Keep this book. Mark it. Bookmark pages. It is to be used as a resource to get you started.

I will not be spending a lot of time on the "why" of each section. This is not meant to be a motivational book. I will spend most of our time together going right into the "how" of it all. Because that is what I have found most business books for stay-at-home moms lack. Every book seems to excite moms to get started, but hardly any books actually tell you step-by-step instructions on how to get started.

And that's why you have this book isn't it? You want to know "how" because you already know "why."

How much work and time will this take from my family?

Life is too complicated not to be orderly.
—Martha Stewart

Balancing work and family is a struggle for most mom entrepreneurs.

The controversial debate over the following question is raging more intensely than ever: "Can moms have it all with work and families?"

I don't understand why that question is so controversial. Of course they can.

I do it every day. It's not easy, but it's definitely doable and gets easier every day.

How often should you work on your business? How much time should you be spending with your kids every day? Those are all ridiculous questions because of the fluidity of a mother's schedule.

Some days you can get 30 minutes in, other days, 8 hours –most likely when your children are a little older.

Back in the day, before electricity, mothers didn't sit all day with their children and plan activities. I don't know where this idea came from–probably a man.

Women worked. Men worked. Families worked. Most families had a farm and the men were farmers while the women took care of the cooking, cleaning and smaller labor duties. I'm not sexist, I'm just speakin' the truth.

Women didn't put off the laundry to have activity day with the kids. The women did the laundry while the kids played outside.

Since then, innovation has happened. Men started creating tools to make farming easier. Factories were made to make everyone's lives easier. Washing machines, refrigerators, light bulbs, telephones and more were created and everyone could finally relax and not do so much work.

Now, everyone seems to work; it's just different work. Women should continue to work too, but now we have the luxury of choosing the work we love, doing it from home, then hiring out the work we don't like so much.

Balancing between work and family is a fluid line and just needs to be checked and adjusted frequently.

Understand that getting your business up and running will always either cost time or money.

The good news is, if it costs you time, it won't cost as much as it used too. I've made the mistakes—too many mistakes, and you can learn from my mistakes, which will ultimately save you a lot of time.

You might be surprised at how quickly you can get a business up and running by just spending a couple of hours a day on it. You'll soon be slowing down to just 4 hours work a week and outsourcing the rest.

Personally, I spent 16 hours a day for the first 5 years to get my business going and this was a huge mistake.

After reading *The 4-Hour Work Week* by Tim Ferris, I realized that I should have been hiring independent contractors to help with the workload. That's not so I could relax, but so I could expand my business even further, then hire out even more. It's a fantastic cycle.

Once you use all your time, you are tapped out. You can no longer expand. You are the only employee in your business and you have no time to expand. You are simply maintaining—running on a treadmill.

This is not my ultimate goal for you. As soon as I realized my mistake, I automated everything and hired two assistants. After that I had oodles of time and found that I was spending only 20 minutes a day answering customers' emails and I had the rest of the day to myself.

Automating a business so it runs by itself is doable and necessary if you don't want to run out of batteries. This is the other reason 9 out of 10 businesses fail. Automating your business requires a whole other book to write. But every business is able to be automated, as long as you let me get my hands on it and help you when you get to that point.

Suffice it to say, working 16-hour days was unnecessary and I kick myself for not learning automation procedures as soon as I started being successful.

The moment you are working more than you'd like, read *The 4-Hour Work Week* and learn how to expand your business whilst shrinking your work hours. I don't dare summarize it here. Tim Ferris is the real master of this.

Before you are ready to scale back though, you'll have to grow your business and learn to balance that fluid line between parenting and work.

I really don't want this book to be about balancing and keeping a schedule. I want it to be the meat and potatoes of starting a business. So let me add a simple tip if you're struggling with balance, then we'll get started with your business.

PowerHomeBiz.com—tagline "Learn How the Big Boys Do It," published an article with tips for at home parents balancing work and family. Here are a few bullet points from the article that may help with anyone struggling with the infamous balancing act of work and family.

- Keep the right perspective.
- Develop a business mindset.
- Make your kids understand the importance of your business.
- Get your family's commitment.
- Be flexible.
- Set what you want to accomplish during the day.
- Consider the needs of your kids.
- Plan frequent breaks.
- Wake up early or go to bed late.
- Set up a dedicated work space.
- Arrange play dates with friends.
- Keep your weekend free for your family.

SUMMARY

Check and adjust the fluidity line of family and work frequently. It's ok to work. Women have worked all throughout human existence. Find a way to adjust yourself and your family to a home business just like you already adjust for everything else that pops into your life.

2 Moms Shocking the World

I like thinking big. If you're going to be thinking anything,
you might as well think big.

DONALD TRUMP

A recent report in The New York Times focused in on the increasing number of moms shocking the world by starting their own successful home-based business. Here are some examples from the article.

Jennifer Fleiss is the co-founder of Rent the Runway, an online dress rental service. She now has 2.5 million members and gave birth to a daughter at the end of last year.

Carley Rooney is 43 and the co-founder of the publically traded media company, the XO Group. She has three children, but her company is valued at $300 million.

Divya Gugnani is the founder of Send the Trend, an online destination for beauty accessories. Divya has both given birth to a baby son and sold her business to QVC already this year.

These Moms weren't born with their business licenses attached to their foot. They had to start somewhere, just like you have to start somewhere. The only difference between you and them is that you are starting now and they are already a few years into their company's lifespan.

The report went on to reveal a shocking statistic that 39 is the average age for people in the US to start their first business. You are never too old to start your own business. And you are never too 'mom' either!*

Becoming shockingly successful does not require a specific personality trait or trust fund, and Tamara Monosoff from Entrepreneur.com dispels 5 myths about what it takes to be a successful mom entrepreneur.

Myth No. 1: You Have to be "Ms. Personality"

Reality: People with many different personality types have become successful. For as many outgoing Martha Stewarts and Richard Bransons, there are countless successful entrepreneurs with very low profiles who wish to stay that way.

Myth No. 2: The Idea is the Most Important Thing

Reality: Yes, it's important to have a good idea. But that's not even half the battle. More important is how you position your product or service, and how it meets your target market's needs.

Myth No. 3: Success Means Never Going Backward

Reality: Yes, successful people are committed to making their vision happen. But they are also willing to change direction.

Myth No. 4: Only Risk Brings Reward

Reality: Any entrepreneurial venture involves some risk, yes. But you don't have to risk everything in order to find success.

---

* http://www.nytimes.com/2012/06/10/business/ nurturing-a-baby-and-a-start-up-business.html?_r=2& pagewanted=1&seid=auto&smid=tw-nytimes

Myth No. 5: Your No. 1 Priority Has to be Money

Reality: For many entrepreneurs, millionaire status is a by-product of their original goals.*

I am not a millionaire and I don't know if I ever will be. But I continue to grow and build new business plans for new businesses so that I continue to feel that initial "success shock" that I felt when my first business reached its first success marker.

Ironically, that first success marker was also the most embarrassing moment of my life.

When I launched my stationery company, it took off so fast that I was actually concerned my wholesaler, Stylart, would find me too demanding.

One day I received a call from a woman at Stylart who said she had been assigned to be my personal representative.

"Did I do something wrong?" I asked her. "Am I that much of a trouble maker that someone has to be assigned to deal with my demands?"

I'm sure I sounded like a 12-year-old girl to this giant company. I was 26 and fresh out of college. She was shocked and said that the situation was the exact opposite. I was giving them so much business that I was now one of their top 5 dealers out of thousands.

The representative said Stylart saw me as an important client and that they were keen to ensure my needs were met. They wanted to help me grow my business and were far from upset with how demanding I'd been.

Now it was my turn to be shocked. I didn't realize I had climbed so high. And what's more I'd done it all by myself from my kitchen table.

---

* http://www.entrepreneur.com/article/178024

She went on to explain that my success had grabbed the attention of their parent company and they wanted to fly a rep out to wine and dine me.

Are you kidding me? I'm that important? But I'm just a mom, with a 2-year-old, in an 800 square foot condo.

They hadn't said where or when the rep would show up, but I figured he would call me at least 24 hours in advance.

He didn't!

Imagine coming home from a week-long vacation with your family and whilst bringing in all the luggage from the car, your 2-year-old manages to open the suitcases and throw every single piece of clothing, make-up and underwear onto the floor and over every piece of furniture.

Our place was so small that the whole living area, including the kitchen sink, was visible from the doorway. We had been in such a rush to get out of the door that we left all the dirty dishes piled up to the ceiling before setting off several days earlier. (Something we would never do now.)

My 2-year-old hadn't slept well in the car on the 7-hour drive home and was rowdy and uncontrollable.

Just then my phone rang.

"Hi, it's Brian from The Occasion Company. I'm around the corner and ready to see you."

"Um . . . Ok," was all I could muster as I continued bringing things in from the car.

I didn't know how to say "no" at the time, especially as this person had flown out especially to see me.

He came to the door and, against my better judgment, I opened it, revealing the circus. Needless to say, the man was shocked.

First of all, this man was expecting to see a fine stationery brick-and-mortar shop. He was also expecting to meet a staff of 10 to 20 people. This man had been in the stationery industry for years and had never seen a situation like this. Imagine Fashion Designer Carson Kressley expecting to walk into Hallmark and instead walking into the Heck home on The Middle TV show and after a category 5 hurricane.

Yeah, that's exactly what happened. We both had no idea what to do or how to act. I couldn't even offer him a seat because there was dirty underwear all over the couch!

I kept looking at the dirty underwear, wondering if I should move it or stand there and hope he doesn't see it.

So we just stood in the middle of the room chatting. He kept asking me in shock, "Where is your staff? It's just you? You do it all? From where? Your computer? You really do it all by yourself?" He didn't believe me.

Following that experience, he continued to be my personal rep and frequently flew out to Las Vegas for visits. Although he did agree to start meeting me at fancy restaurants and I got a babysitter.

It's fun to be wined and dined. We became great friends and I dare say he liked me more than some of the other companies he had to visit because it was just me, and I was a joking, informal mom.

You will be in the same situation, depending on the industry you go into. Let your numbers get the big boys' attention. You don't need to shout things, scramble or feel intimidated in any way because your work and numbers will do the talking for you.

You too will also soon be wined and dined, and if you're in an industry without reps, then wine and dine yourself when you reach your goals.

As mortified as I was by what happened, this experience, to me, marks my first success as an official business, though thankfully it wasn't my last.

I wish someone would have told me these tips to keep the professionalism in business without sacrificing family or adding pretense. Don't apologize for your kids. Mommy Millionaire Kim Levine also talks about this in her book *Mommy Millionaire*. We need to stop apologizing for our kids' squawks and energy while we're on the phone or in meetings. Kids are kids and they don't understand the seriousness of the situation. If anything, we all take situations too seriously and need to lighten up to the same degree as our children.

Don't pick up the phone. During the day, if my kids are rowdy or particularly energetic and the phone rings, I just don't answer. If it's going to cause you anxiety, stop answering it all together. If it's important, the person will leave a message or contact you via email. Or, if you're like me, you can get a free online chat system for your Website at craftysyntax.com. You can pay someone at elance.com or guru.com to install it for you for $30 - $100 depending on the Web programmer's location.

Add a disclosure to your answering machine message. I include the disclosure on mine that says the quickest way to reach me is through live chat or email. So everyone who calls me understands this is my preferred method of communication. Email is quickly becoming everyone's preferred method of communication anyway, so we all have a paper trail and can stay organized.

Say no and don't apologize for it. I should have said 'no' to Brian when he asked if he could stop by. If you ask him, he would probably say he wished I'd said 'no' too. He did not know that I was a stay-at-home Mom and that was my own fault for not explaining that. He probably felt like an intruder and I felt like a fool. You can say 'no' to lots of things like PTA meetings and extra bake sales for your kids' schools too. When you say 'yes' to those things, you are saying 'no' to your business. You have to think of your new business as if you are your own boss. Would you ask your boss for a day off so you can go sell cupcakes at your kids' school? Probably not. If it's that important to you to sell baked goods, do it. But if you feel too overwhelmed to do both, then you have to choose.

Pick a neutral location. If you need to have business meetings in person, I suggest choosing a neutral place like a coffee shop. Don't allow them to come to your home and, if you can avoid it, don't go to their office. If you are negotiating, this can give them a home field advantage.

Just say it. I continue to go to trade shows and when I tell companies I work out of my home, they seem to give me an indifferent attitude and quickly move on to chatting up a brick-and-mortar owner. I remember this and take my business elsewhere. It's their loss and that loss will grow and grow as more and more multimillion dollar businesses are started from homes. I don't pretend that I own a brick-and-mortar store and I don't avoid telling them I'm a stay-at-home mom. In fact, I purposefully tell them to gauge their reaction. This will immediately tell me if I want to go into business with them. It is harder to find those companies that are willing and warm to working with stay-at-home mom businesses, but when you find them, they are golden. Spread the word about those companies to help them too.

As you grow your business, you will want to gauge your success and mark those memories for later. This helps you to remember how far you've come.

Sometimes your business grows at such a steady pace that it's hard to remember all of the growth along the way.

Just like your kids might have a growth chart, your business should too.

When I first started out, I had a $500 a month goal, then I moved up from there.

I have always wanted to have a $10,000 month since I worked at a multi-level marketing company way back when. It seemed a little farfetched to me, but I kept trying. I told myself that if I achieved it, I would buy myself an award and have it engraved. It seems like such a silly incentive, but I wanted an award even if I had to buy it for myself.

January is the busiest month of the year for wedding stationers, so every January I knew I had to try my hardest to reach that goal. For a few years, I got really close to $8k, but I could not get near my $10k goal. I kept trying.

Finally, in 2010, something snapped. No more playing around. I was going to spend every ounce of my energy up-selling and marketing to get past that $10k.

I didn't even want to count anything up until after January was over.

I was shocked when I did the numbers. I not only surpassed my goal, I made $13k. I couldn't believe what I was looking at. I crunched the numbers again and checked my business bank account to be sure. When I was sure of the accuracy in accounting, I was so excited that I went out and bought that engraved award for myself! I added my husband's name to the award too since I could not have done it without his help with the kids and some serious house cleaning.

Set a starting goal to reach $100 in a month then treat yourself to a mani-pedi and a nice dinner when you reach it. Continue to increase your goals from there, but don't let goals distract you from doing the actual work of growing your business. If you grow your business properly, the money will follow.

SUMMARY

Shock yourself every step of the way during your business growth. Moms are shocking the world every day by becoming millionaires and they weren't born that way. Most of them had to start from scratch just like you and me. Say 'no' and don't pretend to be a different type of company. Say that you are a stay-at-home mom running a business and let what happens happen. Set new goals and reward (award) yourself when achievements are met.

3   Your Breaking Point

The only way around is through.
—Robert Frost

Every business owner reaches a hesitation point in their business. Many quit at this moment, some take a break and some keep trudging along. Let's talk about the reason each of these groups either quit or keep going. Then we'll go through the reasons for you building your business and the motivation it will take to get to the automation point we talked about in the previous chapter.

As mom entrepreneurs, we are always forced to face and deal with obstacles that others in the workforce don't. Many moms come to a point where those obstacles become deal breakers for owning a business. The only way to continue your business is to change your mind-set to "in spite of," instead of using those obstacles as excuses.

Say, for example, you own a consulting company that requires a lot of time on the phone. You already see where I'm heading with this. Your kids have a natural instinct to know exactly when you get on the phone and start to fight, cry or need your attention at that exact moment. So is running the consulting company impossible? Do you quit and say "I couldn't do it because the kids cry every time I'm on the phone"? Or do you instead say "I'm going to do it anyway, in spite of the fact that my kids cry every time I'm on the phone"? Whatever your excuse is, if you change it into "in spite of" you can then change your whole outlook on your business. Perhaps you exchange babysitting times with the neighbors for an hour every once in a while. Or perhaps you develop an online chat system so you can avoid the phone all together—which, by the way, is amazing and what I did.

Other obstacles will also inevitably arise that are completely unexpected. The death of a loved one, your spouse being laid off, or even your kids simply needing you because of a mental or physical illness.

I had a roommate in college, Kara, who started a wonderful life after marrying her prince. She had no idea her life was about to be turned upside down as she had one child that was stillborn and another child that suddenly became injured and could no longer walk, play games or even color pictures. The injury could have claimed her little boy's life. Soon after that, she found out her husband had to go in for major surgery himself. She now needed a special van and a permanent nurse for her little boy. Her husband was attending school and the world was on her shoulders. I'm sure Kara had many sleepless nights crying, but she never let anyone know. This is when she came to me and asked me to help her start a crochet business. I was shocked and thought "how will she ever find the time with the world on her shoulders?" But then I realized, she had an "in spite of" attitude. She was going to start a business in spite of everything she was going through in the hopes that it would help her little family become one again. She can't take a lot of orders at once, but she grows her business tiny bit by tiny bit, hoping that it can contribute even the smallest bit to her family's welfare. She also crochets the cutest items ever. Kara's crochet shop can be found on Etsy at http://KaraLynDesign.etsy.com.

Sometimes your hesitation and excuses are simple things that just get under your skin.

Every business I've built up has a hesitation moment. Yours will too. What will get you through it? You need to come up with your big "Why?" Why are you building the business in the first place? You cannot give a wimpy answer to this question or it will not stand up to the hesitation that will come your way—and it will come your way.

If you cannot come up with a strong "Why", then you've found the wrong industry or you shouldn't be in business at all. Why is it so important to you? Why this business? Why now? Why you?

When you get to that hesitation moment, it will be easiest to get through it if you can:

1. Identify the hesitation moment
2. Take an hour break and possibly even sleep on it
3. Get to the "Suck it Up" phase of thinking.

The "Suck it Up" phase of thinking is when your kids spill nail polish on the carpet or red Kool-Aid on your silk curtains.

You've been there.

At first you cringe.

Eventually, you get to the "suck it up" phase of thinking and clean it up. Do I need to expound further? I think every mom knows what I mean by this.

One of the best things you can do after sucking it up is to "Attack Your Frog" as Tsh says on SimpleMom.net. She suggests, "After your morning routine, attack that one thing you dread the most."* What are you avoiding? Now do it anyway and do it first.

Soon, you will be making enough to automate your business and hire assistants to do the tasks you can't stand. But for now, you're

---

* Source: http://simplemom.net/7-ways-to-find-motivation-at-home/

going to have to do the dirty work. Get in the trenches and do it as fast as possible.

The site e.ggtimer.com does wonders for me to get through these phases. I set the timer and race the clock on my computer to get through any dreaded tasks.

If you're in a business you love, that's great, but every business has an aspect that they hate. It can be accounting, billing, invoicing, customer service or something else. Whatever it is, suck it up and get through it until you can outsource it.

Remember your "why" and the hesitation and suck it up moments will be a lot easier to handle.

SUMMARY

Every business must overcome obstacles. When you hesitate you must have your firm "why" lodged in your heart and mind or you will quit altogether. Get through the tough times as quickly as possible, then outsource when you can afford it.

4 Exclusively for Blog/ Vlog Businesses

*It should feel genuinely good to earn income from your blog —
you should be driven by a healthy ambition to succeed.
If your blog provides genuine value, you fully deserve
to earn income from it.*
—STEVE PAVLINA

After I started dozens of companies for myself, friends and family, I started my blog RichMomBusiness.com. I quickly learned that blogging as a business is harder than the dozens of companies I built up before it.

It's more difficult because Google AdSense and other affiliate links don't bring in as much revenue as you'd think, so you have to make your own products to sell and supplement what AdSense and affiliate links don't bring in anyway. So why have a blog in the first place if your whole desire is to create products?

You can have a blog as a news system for your company featuring new products, sales and discounts. But I strongly suggest you don't start a blog about the art world as a whole if you just want to sell some art.

Sometimes business owners go too far down the wrong path by creating two separate businesses and not realizing it. They create a blog about arts and crafts, expecting themselves to blog daily and all they want to do is sell their beaded necklaces.

The reason I continue to blog and vlog myself is simply because it's become a sick addiction that I have fallen madly in love with. Otherwise, I would have quit and just sold my products the same way I did for my first dozen businesses.

Blogging/vlogging is a ton of work with little to no reward, except an occasional thank you from your readers/watchers. This is why 90% of bloggers quit within the first three months. Those bloggers usually start by reading a book that said they could get rich by writing a few opinions on a blogspot blog and the money will come rolling in.

It just doesn't work like that and here's why.

As a journalist major in college, we were required to take full-time classes about newspaper ethics and why newspapers themselves don't sell products. They sell advertising. Newspapers don't sell affiliate products. Their products are their stories. They want to write good stories because it brings more readers and, in turn, those ads get views and their paying advertisers are happy.

Other magazines like National Geographic charge a subscription fee so they don't have to bring in advertising at all. Subscribers are happy because they hate looking at ads and National Geographic is encouraged to write good articles and take good pictures to bring in the subscription fees.

All of a sudden, there is a grey line introduced in the world when blogs enter the picture. Bloggers don't always understand that it's the well-thought-out, researched content that brings the readers and ultimately the ads. They also don't understand that affiliate links shouldn't be thrown out in every article to try to make money. People sniff that stuff out and walk away.

I'm not against affiliate links, even though I prefer not to use them myself.

I know some folks get a lot of money for using affiliate links. I don't think those folks are dishonest because usually they use the products they are affiliates for. I just want to dispel the myth that creating a blog immediately equals success or money. It simply doesn't.

Owning a blog or vlog is extremely similar to owning your own magazine or newspaper. I would know; I ran my high school newspaper, my college newspaper, and eventually, a local Las Vegas weekly newspaper. It's pretty much parallel, except for the fact that I don't have a fabulous copyeditor checking my work for errors.

If you do want to start a blog as your business instead of selling products, great! As long as you're willing to put in the time and work consistently, it can be one of the most rewarding and amazing experiences of your life.

My two big tips for starting a blogging business would be to get a premium account at SocialBuzzClub.com for quick growth and also read ProBlogger by Darren Rowse and Chris Garrett.

If you're going to go with video blogging (aka vlogging), then I suggest obtaining a free subscription to http://www.youtube.com/ReelSEO, http://www.youtube.com/VideoCreatorsTV and http://www.youtube.com/VidiSEO

http://www.youtube.com/jameswedmore on YouTube as well.

Kate Riley was a full time lawyer and had a love for repurposing furniture on a dime budget. She loved it so much that she started a blog about home improvement and design (CentsationalGirl.com). She has fun taking photos of her work and wrote 'how-to' articles with step-by-step instructions which enabled others to learn how to do the same. Kate's blogging became so popular that she now writes for Better Homes and Gardens magazine and was featured on the Nate Berkus show.

Kate quit her career as a lawyer in 2010 and started blogging full time. She now works seven to eight hours per day split between mommy duties and work duties, which include everything from answering emails and carrying out DIY projects, to writing and photo editing. She loves every minute of it and makes enough to put food on the table and help with the mortgage. Kate says, "For me, it's never been about the money. When you love what you do, it's not really 'work.' Don't ever be scared to follow your passion, believe in yourself, invest in yourself."*

SUMMARY

Start a blog for your business as a business news system, but don't start an industry-wide blog just to gain buzz about your products. Start an industry-wide blog/vlog if it's truly your passion. Otherwise, there isn't a ton of money to be made from blogging/vlogging by itself until years down the road after your blog has proven itself and has grown immensely.

---

* http://www.centsationalgirl.com/about/ + a personal email interview on June 26, 2012

5 My Proven Formula Introduction

*Success consists of going from failure to failure
without loss of enthusiasm.*
— WINSTON CHURCHILL

Before I introduce each step in the formula, I would like to tell you how it works and why it's important. I would also like you to know where it came from and how I developed it. Who would want to follow a formula if it lacks any credibility or testing?

A successful business is comprised of many aspects. This formula is as basic as it gets to help your business build momentum. It is crucial that you consider every step and feel its importance or your business won't be as successful as it can be. You will also have trouble automating, expanding or starting more projects if your first business isn't ready to be automated at the switch of a switch (did I really just say switch of a switch)?

However, this formula is not all inclusive. Many more aspects can be added to make a business successful and every day there are more apps, software, and search engine algorithms that change everything. This is a hardy start, though, and it will begin generating some income for you. It is a perfect base to build upon.

I want to go into each area of business in depth before presenting the formula in a bulleted list.

My hope is that by examining each area in depth before presenting the bulleted formula, you'll understand the importance and role of each bullet point of the formula. The bulleted formula can feel quite large at first glance, so if you read how to do everything in depth first, the list might not seem as daunting because you will know how to do each step by the time you get to it.

This is a lot of information and can feel very overwhelming. But don't let it get to you. Just do a little every day and you'll be surprised at how quickly you start your business.

How did I come up with the formula?

After building dozens of businesses for myself and others, I've learned what makes a business tick and what can make a business boom.

Now it is rare for me to start a business which doesn't go on to great success as long as the business owner puts in the work. This is because I use the same formula time and time again that I'm going to give you. I have used this formula personally and when I consult and coach businesses and stay-at-home moms starting businesses, I begin with this basic formula as well.

Jodi Bigler, Bigler Designs, followed my formula. Listen to what Jodi says about it:

"I never thought in a million years that I could make money from this little hobby of mine. Where do I begin? How do I market my products differently so they stand out? How do I set up online shops? Come up with ideas? Business cards, logos, websites, organization and every little thing that one must do before officially passing go? I tossed and turned over the idea of finally selling my crochet items.

"I emailed Renae some photos of my work. After hitting the send button, I was in a panic. Would this work? What would she think?

Could I make myself as successful as she was? When I got a reply saying she was in love with my products and they were some of the best she had seen, I was delighted.

"When she told me she was willing to help, I was ecstatic! With Renae's assistance and expertise, I was able, in a year, to go from being a stay-at-home mom raising two kids with no side income to making over $400 in one day.

"My business has now been open a year and a half, and a day hasn't gone by when I haven't made money from what I do."

Jodi has broken into the local market and now sells to local boutiques first hand.

SUMMARY

I've started dozens of businesses and have learned about success through failure. You will learn the same success, but you won't have to experience the same failures as long as you follow my formula. If you want to find out more about what I do and the companies I run, you can see a list of all my businesses and projects at: www.byrenae-christine.com.

6 Your Idea

Believe you can and you're halfway there.
— THEODORE ROOSEVELT

Before starting a stay-at-home business, you must come up with an idea. Many moms find business ideas from skills they have. Some business ideas are discovered from passions.

Most books tell you to think about your skills, then start a business from there.

I tell you, that's bunk!

I have a skill at eating until my stomach hurts. That doesn't mean I want to start a restaurant. I have a skill at getting my kids to behave in public. That doesn't mean I want to start a company to teach others the skill. (Though if you must know how I do it, check out the Love and Logic Institute).

Instead of inciting skills, think about what you love. You must love it so much that you want to live it.

I loved paper so much that even as a kid I would go to the stationery aisle while my friends and siblings went to the toy section. I did not have a skill at designing. I did not know anything about paper. I was simply a paper snob from birth. Now, even after so many years, I see a piece of letterpress and need to remind myself to breathe.

Beautiful paper pieces make me swoon every time. What makes you physically swoon? That is what you're meant to do.

Skills are easy to acquire these days with YouTube, Lynda.com and easy to find mentors.

Find what you love, then develop the skill if you need too. It might take time. It will be worth it. Besides, if you have a passion for it, then you will love learning the skill anyway.

You might be one of the lucky ones who already have a skill for what you love and want to expand as a business.

Passion is so easily discounted in business discussions among pessimists. In fact, it's practically a swear word among big CEOs at giant companies.

Who cares about passion? They say. Supply and demand! Create what sells!

That way of thinking is over. You constantly see big companies scrambling to get in on social networking and connecting with niche customers. They are struggling. They are dying.

Why?

Because they are trying to reach everyone and so they reach no one. Traditional marketing is dead. In fact, the chief executive of one of the world's largest marketing groups in the world, Saatchi & Saatchi, says management, the Big Idea and strategy are also dead.

Kevin Robert's, Saatchi & Saatchi's CEO, spoke at The IoD's Annual Convention in April 2012 about what is coming in business. His speech proves that the prime market for mothers to create businesses right out of their homes is now.

Roberts doesn't mention mothers specifically, but look at a few bullet points of his talk describing the next generation of successful companies. Tell me this doesn't sound like he's describing his own mother.

"Business leaders need to become creative leaders."

"Leaders need to become emotional thinkers."

"There are three secrets to emotional thinking—mystery, sensitivity and intimacy. It is a lot about story telling."

"Think about how you can build empathy."

"Don't just interrupt, but interact."

"Everyone wants a conversation. They want inspiration."

In his speech, he goes on to describe what makes a company a success. Read on and see why now is the perfect time to start a niche company right from your home that you're passionate about.

"Ideas are today's currency not strategy."

"Our kids are connecting to each other and to brands across the world with no money involved."

"You have to make sure you have dreams and your brand also needs a dream."

"Who wants to be a Chief Executive Officer? It sounds like you work for the government and who would want that? Being a Chief Excitement Officer would be better, don't you think? The role of a good CEO is to get people to buy into their dreams and their company's dreams."

"There are no more big ideas. Creative leaders should go for getting lots and lots of small ideas out there."*

Many of the moms who come to me for help already have a good idea for the type of business they would like to start. They ask my advice on whether their business idea is a good one or not and I can always sense that the real questions they want the answers to are:

- Will this business be successful?
- Will I be successful?
- Can I really do this?

---

* http://www.thedrum.co.uk/news/2012/04/25/marketing-dead-says-saatchi-saatchi-ceo#eZeu1Ewvffv3WPIq.99

Well I have some very good news for you. Even if you want to sell compost from your own backyard, your business will be successful as long as you follow a simple formula for success and you are passionate about your business. (By the way, there is a market for compost.)

The problem with most moms who come to me isn't their business idea at all. It's their self-esteem.

Motherhood is humbling. When you change poopy diapers, clean up every mess and only get dressed on days when the UPS man might swing by, then it's easy to feel underappreciated. It's easy for your self-esteem to take a dive.

But we need to combat this if we're going to expand your vision.

Let's talk about one of the most common thoughts stopping mothers from a successful business: "Why me?"

Surprisingly, many mothers don't ask "Why me" when something bad happens, but rather when or if something good happens. It's that humility issue again.

To be honest, I have felt the same way, so I completely understand the feeling. In fact, I've built dozens of businesses from the ground up and sometimes my husband will still hear me mumbling the question when I get a good review or a bit of praise.

"Why me?" isn't a question you get over easily if you're like me. It's almost like an addiction to feel guilt for being successful while others around you stand still or even decline.

But what if Beethoven had let that feeling stop him? What if the first Dixieland band never played?—Probably only Tom Cote and I would suffer because we're the only listeners on that Pandora station. (Shout out to Tom Cote from the Tom Cote Show on YouTube. I love you!)

But what if Monet never painted his first painting? Or Michael Phelps felt bad that the Olympians in the other lanes couldn't catch up?

You must rise then turn around and help others rise.

I am always telling my 8-year-old daughter that she can be anything she wants to be. She finally came to me with the announcement that it's her 'calling' to be a hairstylist.

"No!" I told her. "You can go to school and you can style hair. But you won't be a hairstylist. You will own a hair salon. You will hire employees who will rent their space and you will get to design the entire place in pinks, purples and sparkles, or anything you like.

"You will sell hair products and hair holders. You can bring your own children into the salon anytime you like and they can play in a real salon, with your own employees, who will dote on them and put ribbons in their hair.

"Your children can dye their hair in pink sparkles every Halloween and be official princesses. You will have a Wii and play center for parents so they can come in with their own children to play with your own children. In fact, you can build a playground right inside the salon if you want. (Just make sure parents sign a quick liability waiver before playing.)

"You will also get your hair styled any time you like and you can take on as many or as few clients as you like."

My daughter's vision was expanded and she simply said. "Yes, Mom, you are right. I will do that."

Of course, she will have to start where everyone starts. She will go to a beauty school, pass her classes and pay her dues at a salon like everyone else. The only difference is that she will take it a step further purely because of choice and because her vision was expanded.

Think of your idea. Yes, it's probably a good one. Every vision is expandable, as long as your skill is teachable and there is a market for it. We will go into more detail about market research in a bit, but first we need your mind to think about your idea properly.

Now expand your vision the way I expanded my daughter's vision. Go wild. Don't worry about specifics or even if it's a possibility right now. After all, if Steve Jobs mentioned the iPhone 20 years ago, he would have been committed.

Now imagine being at your expanded version of your idea in five to ten years. That might seem like a long time. If it takes ten years to get there, will it be worth it? Only you can decide that.

Your journey is about to begin and five years from now you could easily be in the same position as me with 2 assistants running your entire business and you making funny YouTube videos, er . . . spending your time how you like.

Remember this day and mark it on your calendar 5 years from now.—Google Calendar is good for this. Think of how happy you'll be if in exactly five years you are running your own business or even several businesses. If you do nothing, nothing will happen, and in five years' time you'll really be kicking yourself when you look at that calendar. Start today.

Your idea should be easily explained in a one or two sentence elevator pitch. If you can't explain it in one or two sentences, keep thinking or change the idea. One or two sentences are all you really get to sell a product to customers, investors or bloggers if you want them to review your products on their site.

In fact, I personally had someone trying to pitch an idea to me once and when I had to explain the idea to another investor, I had no idea what the product even was and had to hang up with that investor to call the initial person back to ask. She still couldn't tell me. The deal went cold because of the lack of 2 sentences.

SUMMARY

Skills should not be the sole criteria for building a business. Check your passion level for your business idea. Now is the perfect time to build a stay-at-home business. Expand your passionate business idea until you feel like bursting with happiness. Start your business today by marking your calendar 5 years from now.

7 Market Research

Some people say, "Give the customers what they want."
But that's not my approach. Our job is to figure out
what they're going to want before they do."
—STEVE JOBS

In my mind, your idea is in one of three categories:

1. Your idea has been done before and there's a lot of demand for it
2. Your idea has been done before and the market is quite saturated
3. Your idea has never been done before.

I have good news. No matter which category your idea falls in, your idea can flourish and be created into a sound, legitimate, fantastic business that you love.

I can already hear your question. "What? How can an idea succeed in a saturated market Renae?"

That's what this book is for.

It's important to recognize and determine supply and demand and not just for today. It's important to try to determine if supply will outreach demand in the near or even far future.

This isn't to determine whether or not your business will succeed, fail or if you should even get into that industry in the first place. It's so we know what strategies to take to make your business work for you whether your market is saturated or not.

Allow me to explain.

Your idea has been done before and there's a lot of demand.

If your idea has been done before and there's a lot of demand for it now and probably in the near and far future, then you can easily see what other similar companies are doing and you can be confident all you need to do is shoot for a higher par in customer service or product quality and you'll be in business forever.

However, this also means that if you come out of the gates with a subpar grand opening, subpar products and subpar customer service, then you can easily be branded as the subpar company compared to the others. This branding can remain for the rest of your company's existence unless you do something awesome-sauce to change that initial impression, which can be extremely difficult.

If your business has a ton of demand and not a lot of suppliers, sometimes that can also be a sign that to run a business in that industry can be a serious headache. If you have a feeling in the pit of your stomach that you can't handle the type of customers the industry brings or if it requires manual labor that you aren't sure about or any other type of concern that makes you hesitate, then think long and hard before you want to go into that industry. Because in this case, the most difficult part of business isn't bringing in customers or dealing with competition. The most difficult part is fighting with yourself to continue. I've been there. I would rather deal with competition in an oversaturated industry than pep-talking my own dragging feet.

If your idea has been done before
and the market is quite saturated

You can still make an extremely successful, awesome-sauce business even if the industry you want to go into is extremely saturated. It requires a little more ingenuity, but it's definitely doable. If it's your passion, you'll have fun doing it too.

In order to succeed in a saturated market, you need to take the business idea and expand it on behalf of the customer. For example, find something to add or improve upon that isn't normally offered in that industry that the customer would love. The customer might not even know they want the improvement. Steve Jobs himself said that he hates Market Research. "Measuring emotional response should be central, not peripheral, to pre-testing." (Orlando Wood, innovation director, BrainJuicer)

The electronics industry is a great example of an oversaturated market, yet Apple continues to find ways to intrigue customers. Then the Android companies soon follow suit. Be the Apple of your industry, even if you're just crocheting hats and scarves.

How can you reinvent that product? Don't just use a pattern someone gave you, invent one yourself.

I just recently bought a crocheted hat that came with a crocheted beard for my YouTube videos, —best investment for my videos ever (though some of my viewers might disagree).

I'm still waiting for someone to crochet a hat with a mustache so I can snatch that up too.

Look at trends and integrate those trends into innovative new products for your industry before anyone else does.

Truth be told, the hardest part about running a business in a saturated market isn't finding customers, it's dealing with the icky companies who copy your every move. (Hint hint to some of you copying my invitations on Zazzle!)

If your idea has never been done before

This category can bring the most risks and rewards of all three categories, especially if you have truly fallen in love with your idea and others love it too.

If you bring your idea to your friends and family and they love it . . . then forget that they love it. Move on to showing your idea to perfect strangers who don't care about you. If those strangers love it, then you might have a real winner. If those strangers have some criticisms, even better! That means that they like your product enough to request improvements.

Yes, it totally stinks when strangers give you criticism on a product that you spent so much time developing and falling in love with yourself. It feels like they are ripping out your heart, pouring gasoline all over it and throwing it into an already exploding volcano. Woosh!

Simply steel your reaction and heal your wounds on your own time. The only reaction you should have face to face with these people is "what else?" Even though it will feel unnatural and you might be fighting back tears or the desire to punch someone in the face.

The risks for this category can be significantly lessened as you talk to more and more people and continually redevelop your product until that fateful day when someone claims they cannot live without your product.

I've had that happen and it's like having your dream celebrity serenade you in person while you soak in a jetted tub with a soap that makes you lose 20 lbs. just by smelling it. (Hint hint Nellie from Hello Gorgeous Bath. It can be cotton candy flavored).

Don't guess which of the three categories above your business belongs too. If you do, your business might be headed toward disaster before you talk to your first customer.

Remember that staggering statistic that 9 in 10 businesses fail? Guessing is one of the biggest reasons why.

So how can we figure out which category your business idea belongs too? It's easier than you might think and won't cost you a penny.

If you can find out what people are searching for on Google, then scope out your competitors, you'll have a pretty good idea of the supply versus demand, don't you think? Wouldn't it be cool if there was a free tool you could use to see what people are actually searching for on Google?

There is. I use it daily.

You'll need a free account on seobook.com to use it, but it is an honest, reputable site that won't spam you to death. In fact, the only reason they make folks get a free account now is because their own tool was being spammed and they got tired of it.

After you login and go to the URL I'm about to give you, simply type in a generic key term to see how many people are searching for your product or idea. You'll see a lot of columns, but don't let that scare you. There's only one column that you should be paying attention too: "overall daily est" which stands for overall daily estimated searches from Google, Yahoo and Bing. Pretty valuable eh?

http://tools.seobook.com/keyword-tools/seobook/

I provide more insight on how to use this tool properly in the SEO chapter, but for now, we're just using it for research.

If your search term doesn't show up at all, try using some variations of your key term. If nothing comes up or the number of daily searches is less than 20, then there's either no demand at all for your business idea or you're in the third category we've been talking about and your industry hasn't even been invented yet.

If you've searched for something so generic that the searches come back with more than 1,000 searches a day, then you need to narrow down your niche a bit. The competition for "weight loss" is staggering and surprisingly enough, it doesn't yield the results that you would think. I'll explain why in the SEO chapter coming up.

If you look at the number of daily searches for your industry, narrow down the niche and it's higher than 20 searches, then it's time to look at your competition to determine if you're in category one or two that we've been talking about.

How do we scope out the competition? Go right to google.com and do a search yourself for the search term you just researched. Don't despair if you see "2,000,000 search results." That doesn't mean that there are 2 million companies to compete with. That just means that those keywords were found in 2 million sites.

You'll really want to dive in here, especially in the listings on the first two pages found on Google. Disregard the paid sponsored listings. We're only interested in the natural search results right now.

This is normally when people get really depressed and rightfully so. You are looking at full-blown companies, your competitors, and your own company doesn't even have a website yet.

Fight the depression and keep looking. What colors are they using? What fonts and styles? What does their branding and packaging look like? How big are their pictures? Are there any features about their sites or products that you love or that you feel you could improve on your own site?

You are doing this research not to copy them, but to make a superior product. You don't just want to one-up them. That would be too easy for them to roll their eyes and copy you. Then you're on even ground. You want to 10-up them. What are they offering and how can you make it 10 times better?

I'm not talking about giving products away or breaking your wallet. I'm talking about the entire user experience. Does the customer have to go through 4 pages just to checkout? Could you change that so it's an instant checkout? Does the customer have access to view colors, styles and other fun options for a product? Are there easily accessible tabs to do that or does the customer have to open a new window as a pop-up?

All of these questions might seem small, but it's a huge different between gaining loyal customers who come back because of the ease of your site and folks fleeing to your competitor who might charge a couple pennies less.

All of this studying can help you to not only create an amazing product, but amazing packaging, branding, customer loyalty and an all-around amazing user experience.

SUMMARY

Research what folks search on Google, then search that term yourself and study your competitors. Figure out which of the three categories your product or idea belongs too. Create an amazing user experience so you are ahead of the competition and they can't catch up.

8 | Legalese Made Easy

Look well to this day. Yesterday is but a dream and tomorrow is only a vision. But today well lived makes every yesterday a dream of happiness and every tomorrow a vision of hope. Look well therefore to this day.

—Francis Gray

When filling out your business license paperwork, you'll come across a section asking you what type of business formation your company will be.

The most common formations of small businesses are Sole Proprietorship, Limited Liability Corporation and/or Partnerships.

A Sole Proprietorship is the easiest to set up. However, if someone ever sues your company, they are actually suing you personally as well because with a Sole Proprietorship you are, in effect, claiming yourself as your company.

A Limited Liability Corporation is more difficult to set up. I suggest utilizing a lawyer if this is the option you choose. There are also various legal websites which can assist you in creating an LLC. One of the biggest reasons small businesses choose to deal with LLC headaches is because of the protection they afford if someone sues your company. The liabilities can stop at the LLC, instead of moving on to your personal assets. So, in this case, you are separating yourself from your company.

A General Partnership, Joint Venture or Limited Liability Partnership can be popular if you're starting a small business with a partner. With each of these options, both partners contribute materials, assets, time and talents equally to the business, unless otherwise stated in their partnership agreement. Both parties also reap the rewards or failures that come with their small business venture.

I personally prefer a Sole Proprietorship, even though I've had an LLC at one point. I've had accountants and lawyers tell me that LLCs don't always stop the liabilities at the business level.

I'm not a lawyer or an accountant, so I'm not sure which lawyers and accountants to believe. Either way, I personally go with Sole Proprietorships and then cover my bases with as many contracts and other legalities as possible so that lawsuits never come my way in the first place.

Don't worry about making a decision on the business formation right away. This decision isn't set in stone. If you start with a Sole Proprietorship, you can always change it to an LLC and then back again if you need too.

It just requires some paperwork and an aspirin.

I'm surprised by how many moms hesitate to start a home business because they are scared of getting a business license. It's a legitimate concern that usually stems from the fear of the unknown. Let me guide you through what you can expect to calm some of your fears if you are going to go the easy route and choose Sole Proprietorship.

Some cities or counties need you to show up to finish the business license process, whilst others allow you to mail everything in. I'm still waiting for the day we can do it online or by email, HELLO! That should have been integrated 10 years ago.

Either way, the process is still so simple you will kick yourself for not having done it sooner.

In every city, clueless goober people are trying to start businesses. Cities hand out business licenses like McDonald's hands out Happy Meals. Cities deal with those clueless people every day. Most folks are first timers. Because of this, the city workers ask you a couple questions to know what category to put you in, then they give you paperwork. But if that's not enough, they tell you exactly what to do next.

This is exactly what my own visits have been like as a Sole Proprietorship. I've done this at least half a dozen times now in several different Business License Departments.

WORKER: Next!

ME: I need a business license. I'm trying to sell a cotton candy lotion.

WORKER: Ok, you will be in the gifts category. Your business license will be ($**) and you will need to fill out these forms. Are you a sole proprietor?

ME: Yes.

WORKER: Then you will need to go upstairs to file a Fictitious Firm Name. Otherwise known as a "Doing Business As" form. Where are you conducting the business?

ME: In my home.

WORKER: Do you own your home? Or do you have permission if you are renting to have a business in your home?

ME: Yes.

WORKER: You will need to provide a copy of your mortgage or rental agreement to prove that you own or have permission to reside in the home. Will you have big signs around your home for your company?

ME: No.

WORKER: Good, because home residential areas can't have big signs. Are you going to welcome customers to your home?

ME: No. I am doing everything online.

WORKER: Good, because your home is not zoned to have customers. (If you do need to have customers come to your home, you'll have to check with the zoning and planning department in your city to see if there is a checklist you can follow to allow this.) Are you selling something tangible?

ME: Yes, my cotton candy lotion.

WORKER: Then you will need to go to the Department of Taxation for a resale certificate and number.

To sum up, you will need to:

Fill out the papers and bring a copy of your mortgage or rental agreement along with one utility bill.

Have the paper signed by the zoning and planning department. (Tell them you won't have customers in your home and everything is drop shipped to make things easier).

Have the DBA filed.

Go to the Department of Taxation and sign up for a resale certificate. (If you aren't selling a tangible product, you might not need a resale license).

After you have done all that, bring the paperwork back and we'll get your business processed in 6 to 8 weeks.

This might seem like a huge list but it's actually not too bad.

Knock off the tasks one-by-one, like any to-do list. There's no reason you can't finish it up in a single day. Take a day aside and just go at it with intensity and be done with it.

Here's a better looking checklist for you. Again, these items can vary depending on your location:

1. Fill out the business license application (From the business license department).

2. Fictitious Firm Name or DBA filed (Usually a different department from the business license department, but typically in the same building. Ordinarily costs extra).

3. Fill out planning and zoning department paper (The form is usually given with the business license application, but you have to take it to the planning and zoning department, which is normally the same building as the business license department).

4. Child Support Waiver (Usually given with the business license application to make sure you pay your child support payments or don't have any).

5. Resale Certificate (Go to your city or states tax department for this. It's a separate form to fill out and turn in on the spot. On your business license, there's usually a checkbox asking if you have been to the tax department and applied for one.)

6. Bring your ID, copy of mortgage or lease agreement, one utility bill and a checkbook.

Note: Every city business license department varies a little, so your conversation and process might differ slightly, but this is basically what you can expect. Also, those government employees are always unhappy, bored and sometimes think of you as a bug, so go in smiling and give them some chocolate you just happened to find in your pocket—you will be surprised at how happy they become.

SUMMARY

Think of the long process of getting a business license as a scavenger hunt and afford yourself a little chocolate each step along the way.

9 Getting it on Paper

The trick is in what one emphasizes. We either make ourselves miserable, or we make ourselves strong. The amount of work is the same.
— CARLOS CASTANEDA

Most business coaches stress the importance of writing a business plan. Truth be told, I've never written a proper business plan in my life for the dozens of businesses I've helped grow.

Instead, I scribble. I take several pieces of paper and I just start writing whatever comes to my mind about the business. I'll write questions that I need ironed out like "how long does it take to make one of these invitations?" or "what color should we make the logo?" or "should we hire out the SEO this time?"

Eventually, my scribbles turn into rhyme and reason. Then I have my entire business down on paper, though it looks like a giant mess.

Putting everything on paper, especially in the infancy of a business, helps to alleviate a lot of the "choose right now" stress that can build up in your head.

You need to take time to make each decision and if you're busy worrying about remembering all the questions you need to answer instead of focusing on each question one by one, then your choices might be tainted or hurried.

Everyone's scribbles are different because everyone's business is different. But here are some basics to consider when you get out your pen.

We will go over a lot of these aspects in the book so you can strengthen or change your scribbles as we go too.

Product Line

- What are you going to sell?
- How much are you going to sell it for?
- Is anyone selling something similar?
- Will your pricing be similar or will you offer something more so you can charge more?
- Are you making or buying your product to sell?
- Do you need to order raw materials or samples?
- How much do the materials and samples cost to make or buy?
- Do you need any software or equipment to create your products?
- What descriptive words are you going to use for your products?
- What will be your pitch to get people to buy your products?

Packaging and Shipping

- What boxes will best fit your products?
- Where can you buy those boxes in bulk?
- How do you plan to package the product itself?
- What inserts and information do you plan on adding to the package?
- Are you going to ship internationally?
- Which shipping carrier are you going to use and why?
- Are you going to print shipping labels from home or brave the post office each time you need to ship an order?

Customer Service

- What questions do you expect to receive from customers?
- If you receive a question repeatedly is there a copy and paste answer you can give them?
- How are you going to address each customer?
- How are you going to sign each email?
- Are you going to have an email signature?
- What are you going to do or say if a customer is unhappy that their product wasn't received?
- What are you going to do or say if a customer doesn't like the product you sent them?
- What is your return and refund policy?
- Are you going to ask for feedback, reviews or testimonials?

Branding

- What colors is your logo going to be?
- What fonts do you want for your marketing materials?
- Are you going to create your logo, use a pre-made logo or hire a designer?
- What are your business colors?
- Are you going to have a symbol with your logo or just lettering?
- Are you going to brand your packaging materials?
- Do you need an Etsy Banner?
- Do you need Social Media Icons to match your logo?
- Do you need a matching, branded Facebook fan page or twitter page? Pinterest?

Photography

- Do you want a traditional white, grey or black background for your products?

- Do you want a textured background like a grey linen?
- Do you want other props in with your item?
- What camera are you going to use?
- What lighting are you going to use?
- Are you going to put a watermark on your photos?
- Are you going to put any other text on your photos?
- Are you going to photograph any color or product options too?

Bookkeeping

- Are you going to use any software to help you?
- Are you going to hire a Bookkeeper?
- Are you going to use spreadsheets?

Marketing

- Are you going to rely solely on social media?
- Are you going to try to get to the top of Google?
- How are you going to be seen?
- Are you going to send your products free to bloggers in the hopes that they'll review you?

Website questions

- What shopping cart are you going to use?
- Are you going to hire out SEO or learn it yourself?
- Are you going to hire someone to create a Website for you?
- Are you going to use a pre-made template or have something custom made?
- Are you going to have an Etsy shop and a Website?
- How many pages will your Website be?

SUMMARY

Get everything on paper, even if it's just in scribbles. Remember, Harry Potter was created in scribbles. It just needs to be written down to help you stay organized.

10 Finances

Success in business requires training and discipline and hard work. But if you're not frightened by these things, the opportunities are just as great today as they ever were.

—DAVID ROCKEFELLER

Let's talk about funding your company, going into debt and how to figure out finances.

If you're lucky and you have the funding to start your own business without the need for financial help from external parties, then there's nothing to stop you from rolling out your new business very quickly.

However, there are many moms out there who just cannot afford to start a business without taking out a loan or chasing a grant. Those are usually bigger businesses and while there's more risk, there can also be greater rewards.

There are many organizations out there that can provide you with advice and support with financing your business. I highly suggest doing your best not to borrow money, but if you have to, take as much advice as possible to ensure you don't over-borrow and your business has a genuine ability to pay off the debt.

More and more grants are given to online businesses every day and there are 30 different grant organizations who can help with this. Go to http://www.grants.gov and start your search there.

There are also lots of companies offering low-interest loans to help individuals starting up from home, especially for women.

Most grants and loans require that you fill out an application and submit it with a business plan. The more solid your business plan, the bigger the chance to get the loan or grant. You can hire someone inexpensively on Elance.com to help you polish up a solid business plan worthy of investors and it will enhance your chances of success as well.

If you can start your entire company for $1,000 or less, even the financial guru Dave Ramsey says go for it. This isn't necessarily going into debt; it's making an investment so you can continually make money in the long run.

As long as you make smart decisions and plan out your business before you jump in, then you should pay little or no stupid tax in the process as well.

I once worked in a Bridal Shop and I never forgot one phrase that the business owner told me. He said "if you buy it for half of what you sell it, then your business can survive."

We don't need to go over tons of calculators and spreadsheets to see if your business will survive. In fact, oftentimes this is why moms never start businesses in the first place.

Buy low, sell high. Don't buy retail then expect to double it. Find a true wholesaler that does not sell to the public and requires a tax resale certificate. Or find a materials supplier looking to sell to dealers and also not the general public.

Many wholesalers claim to be wholesalers, but sell to the general public themselves at a discounted rate. This undercuts you and also steals your customers.

How do you find good wholesalers and suppliers? My best advice is to avoid searching Google. 99% of the Google searches I've tried are actually retailers masking themselves as wholesalers.

You can find some amazing wholesalers by going to a nearby tradeshow or find a tradeshow database online and search their vendor listings. Check out their websites, products, pricing and then email or call them, asking "Do you sell to the general public"; "Can I sell your products online"; "What are your purchase minimums"; and "Do you need a tax resale number to become a retailer?"

As you build your product line, write down the costs of each material going into the product. Be sure to include packaging costs for the actual item and also shipping for those materials and packaging items to be shipped to you from the wholesalers.

As you develop your product line, enter all of this info into your own spreadsheet or program so you can look to it and easily crunch the numbers each time. I personally have a simple spreadsheet for both product costs and crunching the numbers. It doesn't need to be complicated.

Just make sure you account for materials, any credit card transaction fees, Etsy or other shopping cart fees (if your shopping cart isn't hosted by you on your own website) and shipping costs. The rest is your commission.

Even though you aren't including your time into that calculation, you should be calculating how much time a product will take to create, package and ship.

Think long and hard about how much you should be paid for your time. If you undercut yourself now, you'll never be able to hire assistants later to do your work and nothing ticks customers off more than raising prices on products they love.

If anything, you should start your prices high and if you find you can't sell much after a few months of building your business, you can cut your prices. Folks love a good sale and will still feel your products are valued at the originally listed price.

At the same time, if you have super low prices and raise them, you will lose any customer loyalty you have gained and they won't trust you to keep your prices as is in the future either.

I'm always surprised to see Etsy listings priced so low that it just covers the costs of the materials to build a custom made product. So that person might be getting $3.00/hour and they are fine with that. You shouldn't be fine with that. If you plan on hiring an assistant in the future at $10/hour, then you should calculate $18/hour into the price of the product to cover both you and your assistant when you're ready to automate everything.

Be careful when you choose the packaging for your product. Even if it's a luxury item, it should not be shipped in a heavy glass which will make both your packaging and shipping costs skyrocket. Think light-weight luxury if you're going that route.

SUMMARY

Get grants if you can. Be careful if borrowing money. Keep your calculations simple. Buy low, sell high. Include your time in the price and make sure it's high enough to pay an assistant in the future.

11 Taxes

Whatever the mind of man can conceive and believe, it can achieve. Thoughts are things! And powerful things at that, when mixed with definiteness of purpose, and burning desire, can be translated into riches.

—NAPOLEON HILL

Every tax section of every business book I've ever read says the same thing and that is . . . they say nothing, because everyone's taxes are different depending on their city, county, state and country.

Even Jason Malinak, a Certified Public Accountant and Certified Treasury Professional says in his own book Etsy-preneurship, "I work with the tax code quite often and still learn something new almost every day!"

There's a reason accountants have college degrees and I would rather hire an accountant with a college degree who's spent years studying and learning taxes than trust my own pen after guessing the tax code.

I highly recommend you have a local accountant do your taxes unless you're an accountant yourself. Accountants are worth their weight in gold and are constantly brushing up on new laws that come on the books every year.

There are tax write-offs that you never imagined possible. Your tax rep. will make it worth your while by saving you as much as possible and even getting you a nice refund if it's available. What you pay them is small compared to the money you save or receive at tax time.

However, hiring an accountant does not mean you shouldn't take the time to understand why your accountant is writing up your taxes in a certain way. Ultimately, as Malinak states, you will be responsible if there are errors on your taxes.

If you do want to learn to do your own taxes, I highly suggest reading Etsy-preneurship to learn from the master CPA himself. Malinak also has a ton of products in his Etsy shop including spreadsheets, guides, tools, tutorials and bundles to help you with any and every question you could possibly have. http://jjmfinance.etsy.com

Here are the most common tax write-offs. But you should still talk to your accountant about these. Every business and location can vary.

Home

The space in your home which you dedicate to your office is tax deductible in terms of the area used up in relation to the rest of the house.

Utilities

A percentage of your utility bills can also be tax deductible and the amount you save will be directly related to the area of space you are deducting from your mortgage or rent payments.

Travel

Your business may be home based, but for every mile you travel in relation to business needs, you can deduct the fuel or ticket costs from your tax bill.

Be sure to always make a note of journeys which were business related, even if it's just driving a couple of miles down the road to drop off a parcel at the post office.

Telephone

The first telephone line in any home is non-tax deductible; however, the cost of any further telephone lines can be deducted from your tax bill, like your cell phone bill.

Internet

Ordinarily, it will not be possible to deduct the full amount of your internet costs, as it's fairly clear that some of your usage will be for personal reasons. You should certainly be able to have a percentage of your internet charges deducted from your tax bill though.

Advertising/Marketing

All fees paid out for the advertising and marketing of your business are entirely tax deductible.

Supplies

Keep track of everything you spend on supplies, right down to the smallest paperclip.

As long as you keep receipts for everything and they are all in relation to genuine business requirements, all home office supply costs are completely tax deductible.

Freelance Contractors

If you have freelance contractors working for you, make sure you let them know you'll be sending a 1099 at the end of the year and that they are in charge of their own taxes. I even have them sign something for me saying they understand that they are in charge of their own taxes.

Owing taxes would be an ugly surprise for them.

SUMMARY

Get someone to do your taxes for you to simplify everything and maximize write-offs and deductions. Do your best to understand your taxes before sending them off. This will help you keep your finances in order throughout the year.

12 Security

If you have an online business and important files that pertain to that business, then you need a back-up system. In fact, I suggest you get more than one back-up system.

I personally back-up everything on a large hard drive and then I have mozy.com automatically back up the rest of my computer. Both are important. Here's why.

In 2006, I used an external hard drive to back-up all of my invitation designs. I had a hundred of them and I spent a lot of time on each one. Because the files were so large, I moved them from my computer to the hard drive.

One fateful day that my husband and I still call "the crash of 2006," I simply moved my computer on my desk just enough that the external hard drive crashed to the floor and broke open. There was no way of retrieving my invitation designs.

Every day for exactly one year, the crash of 2006 was mentioned. This is because every day someone ordered an invitation design that I had to painstakingly reinvent from scratch. It was hard enough making the invitations in the first place, but when you have to re-design the invitation to the exact detail, it's harder than designing it the first time because the customer expects an exact duplicate.

I had to work double the hours every single day to reconstruct my entire portfolio.

After that, I started backing up my files on an external hard drive and also on mozy.com.

Then, one fateful day, not too long ago, my daughter's 6-year-old friend was simply drinking water near the computer and spilled the water all over the keyboard. There was no recovery. The computer was ruined.

At the same time I was just putting the finishing touches on a 45 hour work project that my church asked me to do. I was only an hour or two away from delivering the entire project. I had forgotten to back-up these files on my external hard drive, so they were simply gone.

Luckily, I had the sense to install mozy.com on that spare computer along with my work computer so I was able to download those exact files onto my work computer and finish up the project as if the water incident never happened. Now that laptop is a great prop for my YouTube videos.

Alternatives to mozy are dropbox, which I also love, or you can even use Gmail or Google Docs (recently changed to Google Drive).

You also need to protect your Internet line and your computer so that hackers don't come in and steal your information, or worse, steal your customer's information. That's a liability that you don't want in court, especially if your customer's credit card information is anywhere to be found.

My personal favorite protection software is from McAfee. You install it once and it runs in the background of your computer. It keeps your computer free from hackers, viruses and spyware.

Oftentimes, folks who seek out a cheaper security software system experience either Internet connection problems because of firewall issues or they find they've downloaded spyware masked as a security system. So be wary of the cheaper versions and go with an anti-virus system that's trustworthy like McAfee or Norton.

SUMMARY

Don't let your business fail just because you didn't back-up something important. Back everything up twice, once externally and once on-line. Use a trustworthy security system to protect your business and customers.

Easy and Compelling Branding

Hire character. Train skill.
— PETER SCHUTZ

One of the biggest mistakes I've seen stay at home moms do, and I actually did it myself, was to name your business after the product you are selling or the industry you are selling it in. Refrain from the temptation of doing this. I repeat Do NOT name your business after the product you are selling or the industry you want to sell it in. Period. End of story.

I ended up changing my business name several times down the road and it wasted a lot of resources that I'd built up.

Changing your name mid-stream can also confuse customers and make them concerned about the identity of your company. It can create distrust and disloyalty with your customers.

Also, do not name your company after a cliché or catch phrase. You would be surprised at how often those are so easily forgotten, even though you feel they will be memorable.

You want to name your company after yourself, or a made up, generic, easy to remember, word.

One reason to name your business after yourself is to keep the option of expanding your business into other areas. You never know where you'll end up.

A business investor told me before I started my business to name my head company after myself because of this very reason. I ignored his advice and I've paid dearly for not listening.

If you don't want to name your main company after yourself because you may want to sell it down the road, then use an easy to remember, made up word that can mean anything.

Think of huge companies:

Google
Facebook
Twitter
Pinterest
Etsy
Wiki
Yahoo!
Hotmail

The biggest and best are all one easy-to-remember word.

Google now has over a hundred projects in flight—probably more. Google products, news, apps for developers, Google+ etc.

If Google had called itself "Best Search Engine" they would be limited on their new projects or it would be back to new branding.

At the time that Google created itself as a search engine, I doubt they imagined they would be creating a social media platform to compete with Facebook. Facebook wasn't even around back then.

This is why you should name your main company after yourself "Lyn Inc." or after a made-up word that could mean anything, like "Borklito."

Naming your main company after yourself or a made-up word does not mean you are limiting your URL or website to that name. It simply means that's the name that will appear on your customers' credit card statements and at the bottom of your websites next to a copyright sign.

For example, I finally wised up and named my company "by Renae Christine." I've been in the journalism business since high school and there's nothing more sweet to me than my byline next to an article. So I named my business after my byline.

Now, whenever I create a new venture, I add my "by Renae Christine" logo next to it. I have dozens of websites and my "by Renae Chirstine" logo is the only common denominator between them all. Ironically, I have dozens of finished websites and the only one that isn't finished is byrenaechristine.com. I vow to finish it when I'm tired of creating new projects and businesses, which will probably be never.

You might not envision yourself creating dozens of businesses right now, but you never know where you'll be five years from now after you've built and automated your first business.

In addition to having a common denominator between all your business ventures, having a company named after yourself can give it a designer feel.

This is exactly what happened to Jodi Bigler from Bigler Designs. She thought she had to work up to being a designer. She expected to work hard and someday, somewhere, someone would call her a designer and she could use the title.

You'll be waiting a long time if that's what you expect. You have to claim your title yourself.

While searching for your company name, try a search at http://www.uspto.gov/trademarks to see if it's already been trademarked.

You want something original which you can eventually trademark yourself. When you are ready to trademark your name, I suggest going to Elance.com and hire an actual person. I've tried online trademark-type sites and they can get confusing and you never end up getting what you want.

Hire a private attorney to do all the paperwork for you. By the time you are through with trademark and private attorney fees, you can expect to pay between $400 - $800 for your trademark.

Next, let's talk about your logo. Do NOT design this on your own unless you are a professional designer by trade. Do NOT use a logo generator or funny online software to do this for you.

Your logo is the most important aspect of your business online, even more so than the product, because it is what will convince first-time buyers to try out your products in the first place.

You can't gain a following if no one is willing to try it for the first time and they won't try it for the first time if your logo looks outdated, juvenile or incomplete.

In fact, I bet there are instances you can think of yourself where you've seen a juvenile or outdated looking site or logo and you couldn't get off that site quickly enough.

The branding and logo is where I find people spend too little of their time thinking when they start a business.

Focus your initial attention on branding and if you do it right, you should never have to go back to it again. It will help streamline everything you do forever more.

Hire someone to do the logo once, then put the same logo on your website, Facebook page, and marketing materials. You can even make your logo transparent and use it as a watermark if you ever need too.

Hiring a branding specialist can be expensive, but I'm going to show you how you can get your entire business branded on a dime.

First, find a graphic artist on Etsy, Elance.com or Guru.com that you feel is worthy of the task. You should like their previous work and style before you even contact them. Otherwise, your styles will clash and it doesn't matter how many revisions are done, you won't be happy.

Next, your graphic artist will only be as good as your instructions, so let me give you step-by-step instructions on how to know what you want and what to tell the graphic designer you want without being a headache customer yourself:

Think about the feeling you want people to have when they look at your products, website, Etsy store and Facebook page. Do you want them to swoon? Find it edgy? Sassy? Think long and hard because you can't have everything rolled into one.

Are you looking for something luxuriously elegant or something more informal, warm and welcoming?

Write down as many adjectives as you can and then start crossing the ones out that clash.

Are you thinking more vintage or modern? Swirls or flowers?

Write everything in your head. Then start narrowing it down to the most important aspects.

Now that you have a couple of the most important adjectives, you really don't get a choice on the rest.

It's now up to Google.

Google Search your adjectives with "color palette right afterward." If you chose elegant as one of your adjectives, then search "elegant color palette." If luxury was one of your chosen adjectives, then Google search "luxury color palette."

Save the images with the exact colors you like to go with your adjectives so you can show your graphic designer upon being hired.

A luxury, elegant color palette is going to be soft with more neutrals, whilst a modern, informal color palette might have bolder options mixed in with the neutrals.

Next, go to fonts.com and search your adjectives there. Type "Elegant" or "Luxury" in the search box and see what comes up.

Click the fonts you like. You'll see an area where you can actually try the fonts with any wordage you like. Type out your business name and see which fonts you like with your business name. You don't need to buy anything at this point. Just write down a couple of fonts that you like and pass them on to your graphic designer when hired. A graphic designer might have that font on hand or a similar one you like just as much. Be prepared to buy the font if the graphic designer doesn't have the exact one you want though.

Next, you need to find a second font to complement your logo font for your tagline or slogan.

If you choose something crazy swirly like Burgues for your logo, then you need to pick a more traditional font to complement and anchor it.

I suggest something that you have on your own computer, like Helvetica or Arial. Or, try my all-time favorite font that goes with everything—Trajan Pro.

After you start using Trajan Pro, you will notice it's everywhere. It's on billboards, signs and about 75% of movie posters. It's a standard font that screams professionalism and will never go out of style.

Give your designer your narrowed adjectives, 2 different color palettes you like, and 3 different fonts. Then let him/her do the rest.

Make sure your designer sends you .eps files, in raw format from the program they created it in (probably Adobe Illustrator or Photoshop) and a high resolution .jpg file. Also ask him or her for the hex color codes from your chosen color palette. The hex color codes start with a # and can be used to brand standard shopping carts, widgets and apps so that they look like they were created just for your business.

You might not have Illustrator or Photoshop, but you want to have the raw files on hand if you need to hire someone else to create business cards or any other printed material for you, they will need those files to ensure the best quality possible.

Lastly, don't forget to get a copyright release signed by your graphic designer so you can use your new logo on absolutely everything.

There it is. You have your logo and branding. From now on, everything you do will need to fit into your adjectives, colors and fonts. This will not only ensure a consistent and memorable brand, but will also make all of your projects for your company easy. You will never again have to ask "what color should we make that" or "what will that look like"? You know what color to make everything and you know what a finished branded marketing material should look like.

If you're struggling to turn out adjectives and colors you like or if you simply don't have the budget to hire a logo designer, even an inexpensive one, then I suggest purchasing a premade package from etsy.com. One of the most awesome-sauce Etsy shops for all premade logos, graphics and templates is created by Kelly Jane (Kellyjsorenson.etsy.com). Everything in her shop makes me swoon and everything in her shop is worthy of creating a solid business brand. She also happens to charge three times too little, which is good for you, but I continue to lecture her on raising her prices. One day she'll listen to me, so buy up everything soon before she finds herself in this book and triples her prices.

SUMMARY

Your main company name should be named after you or a loved one (like a child), or it could be named after a made-up word—Words With Friends always gives me great ideas while I play. Check trademarkia.com for any trademarks regarding your business name. Spend some time thinking about your branding, the way you want it to feel. Hire out for your logo and never do it yourself unless you're a professional.

14 Photography and product photos

There are no rules for good photographs,
there are only good photographs.

—Ansel Adams

Regardless of the nature of your business, there is one thing that can guarantee that you'll get a lot of interested visitors and higher sales and that's great photographs. Of course the opposite is true if you have horrible photographs. No one will want to buy your products.

It's funny—when I first started out, I used straight on shots. I would put my invitations on a simple background, take the shot, color correct the photos, then put it up on the Web. I was getting plenty of orders, but I wanted more.

I thought if I changed the photography to reflect more creative angles and different artsy techniques for certain parts of the photo that I would get more sales because the products would then be considered designer photographs.

I was surprised when I started getting less orders this way. Customers were annoyed that they couldn't see a straight on shot of the product, especially on the thumbnail images. So did I get rid of the creative shots? No. I used both and started getting even more sales.

The first photo thumbnail that customers click on to enter the product details is the straight on shot. Customers seem to love this best. Then, once they get the straight on shot in their head, they click on the more creative photos. That seems to seal the deal for hesitant customers. They like seeing all the angles, but they always love seeing the straight shot image first.

Now, I can't tell you how much money I've wasted on all these photo boxes and lighting equipment to make a professional studio in my home. It's all garbage if you don't know how to use it—and I didn't. Eventually, I learned about lighting techniques and white balance, which saved my photos and increased sales.

There are entire books written about both these things and I go into more details on my blog, but for now, I'll just give you a few of the top 7 shooting tips I've learned.

1. Do not shoot outside with the sun directly on the product. If you shoot outside, try to do it on an overcast day.
2. You are trying to eliminate as many shadows as possible. However, you can keep some of them for effect. I've learned that most of the time, shadows sneak in anyway. So if you try to eliminate all the shadows, you'll end up with just enough.
3. If it's super sunny outside (like it always is in Las Vegas where I'm at) take your photos by a window, but once again, don't let direct sunlight hit your shooting area.
4. Choose a neutral background that isn't distracting. Grey linen seems to be the most popular for this right now. I like linen, but I have a wooden table that I also use and love.
5. Details. If you notice a flaw while you're shooting and you wonder if anyone else will notice a flaw, guess what? They will see it and wonder if you saw it. Then they'll wonder if you will miss details on their orders.
6. Use a grey card. If you don't know what this is, google it and learn how to use it to calibrate your white balance on your camera.

7. Get an SLR or DSLR camera. I use the Rebel xti and I know a lot of people who use that camera and love it. It's inexpensive and works perfectly for product photos.

If you're going to take your product photos yourself without hiring it out, you need the proper equipment. Do NOT take your product photos with your phone and expect Photoshop to do the rest. Yuck. It doesn't work that way.

I can't tell you how great the photos taken with SLR cameras come out. There's just something so magical about them. Even something as mundane as a cup of coffee and newspaper can look vintage and modern at the same time.

If you are going to photograph your products yourself, I strongly suggest a 7 day to 3 week photography school online. You will use the information you will learn from the photography schools for the rest of your life. Once again, visit my blog for suggestions on short and cheap online photography schools. They can be as cheap as $99, so there's really no excuse for not attending if you're going to photograph your own products. You would probably pay someone more than that to outsource your product photos anyway, so you might as well make the investment and gain the education yourself.

Photography software can get expensive, but it's worth every penny if you can afford it. It will pay for itself within the first year of your business because you won't have to hire a designer to edit your product photos. I suggest Lightroom or Photoshop as your first choices, but there are plenty of others out there.

If you splurge and get Photoshop, I suggest getting a few actions from paintthemoon.net. The Spoonful of Sugar action set is my go to for all of my own video thumbnails on YouTube, and once you visit their website, you'll see why. The Coffee House Yummy

Action set is to die for too (http://paintthemoon.net/blog/buy-pse-compatible-actions/coffeehouse-decaf/).

Be careful when using these actions with your product photos because you want your photos to accurately represent what you're selling. But if you're doing a separate photo shoot with some of your products in the hands of its intended user for ads, blog posts or sales materials, then these are absolutely a must have.

If you've never used Photoshop or action sets before, be sure to watch some tutorials on YouTube before you try it so you don't pull your hair out. They are extremely simple, as long as you educate yourself for 5 minutes before you try it.

PaintTheMoon.net has a whole database of video tutorials to help you as well: http://paintthemoon.net/blog/buy-pse-compatible-actions/coffeehouse-decaf/.

SUMMARY

Take both straight on photos and creative angles. Most shopping carts will allow for multiple photos per product. Learn how to shoot properly or hire someone to enhance your photos for you. If you enhance your photos yourself, make sure you get the proper equipment and software for it.

15 Shopping Carts, Blogs and Websites

The man who will use his skill and constructive imagination to
see how much he can give for a dollar, instead of how little he
can give for a dollar, is bound to succeed.

— HENRY FORD

The biggest mistake I see when folks are building websites from scratch is just that—they are trying to do it from scratch.

When you view a complicated program like Photoshop, you see thousands of programmers' names attached to it and it's been around since 1988. Granted, Photoshop is a computer software program while your website will be an online software program, but the issue is still the same.

The folks trying to build these complicated websites from scratch are always surprised when those programmers charge upwards of $5,000, but it's because they are hiring that company to match just as complicated of a program that's been around and perfected for a dozen years by thousands of full-time programmers.

Instead, you can gain access to a lot of white-label, turnkey programs that were created just for people like you, and are ready to install and brand yourself within minutes. You can own these programs outright and install them right onto your own web hosting without paying monthly fees or even initial fees to use the program.

The perfect example of this, and the one I recommend the most, is called OsCommerce. It sounds complicated and while the website is probably as complicated as Photoshop, it's back-end was designed with you in mind, so it's as easy to use as your toaster oven, or close to it. The best part? It's an open-source project so you get the work of a thousand full-time programmers since March of 2000.

OsCommerce also has a ton of widgets, add-ons and scripts to make it even more customized toward your needs.

How do you get OsCommerce installed? It's so easy to do that you can do it yourself. In fact, I have a video tutorial playlist online on RichMomBusiness.com to help you do it.

The step-by-step tutorials show you exactly how to install, brand and customize the shopping cart yourself. All you need is your own hosting account and URL at bluehost.com, which also happens to be one of my all-time favorite hosting companies because of its amazing support, honesty and limitless capabilities.

Including the cost of hosting at Bluehost, by using OsCommerce and my step-by-step tutorials, you will have your own custom Website/Shopping Cart up and running for under $100.

Another aspect I love about OsCommerce is that you can find hundreds of templates online to brand your store to fit your needs. Templates can be free or really pricey depending on your level of pickiness.

I suggest you be a little pickier on this one. The premium templates are a lot better looking and will generate more sales in the long run. Premium templates can cost around $175. Be careful not to pay $1,000 for a template. Some sites say they will install a template for that price, but you can install it in less than a dozen steps yourself for free and I show you how in the OsCommerce tutorials free.

A word of caution before purchasing a template. OsCommerce has different versions just like Microsoft has different versions. You need to ensure that the template you purchase conforms with the same version of OsCommerce that your Bluehost Account will install.

You can contact Bluehost's live chat to ask which OsCommerce version their hosting has in their quick and easy site builder. After you have that info. you can go shopping! Each template will tell you which version of OsCommerce it is compatible with.

If you are still scared and don't want to install OsCommerce yourself, you can hire someone at Elance.com or Guru.com to install it and your template for you for $50 to $200.

If you go with the option to hire out the installation, here are some tips to ensure your money doesn't disappear and you get the quality work you want.

When you add your project for the bids to start, make the title of your project "Install OsCommerce with Premade Template on Bluehost." This screams one thing to programmers–quick and easy buck. This installation will take them less than 30 minutes to do as long as you've already purchased your hosting and template.

Look for an independent programmer instead of a company. They will be less expensive and usually work weekends and evenings to get projects finished up quickly.

Don't be afraid to hire someone in India, but make sure they understand your project, have amazing ratings and also written reviews.

Watch out if you see five stars on the programmer's projects, but no written review next to it. This is usually a sign that someone hired them, struggled to get the project completed, and gave them a pity 5 star.

The good programmers will have been a member for at least a year with many projects and many 5-star written reviews.

Always ask one or two questions before starting a project. This will help you gauge their reaction time to see if they get back to you at a snail's pace. I usually ask upfront, but simple questions. In this case, I would ask "Have you ever worked with cPanel before to install OsCommerce?" CPanel is just the site management tool Bluehost provides to make your site building easy. It's the easiest site management software out there and it's a no brainer that your programmer will know what it is and how to use it. But again, you're just trying to gauge their reaction time.

In your description ask that the project be finished within 24 hours. Since the project will take less than 30 minutes this should not be a problem and if a programmer says it will take longer, then they are either trying to pull extra money out of you for extra pretend work or they are simply incompetent programming wannabees.

Another software platform that I would strongly suggest if you aren't interested in OsCommerce is Wordpress. This would be a great Blog + Shopping Cart in one option. I wouldn't suggest signing up for a Wordpress account, but rather install it separately on your Bluehost account so it is your own and you can add the widgets and scripts that you like to make it your own.

Once again, Bluehost has the same easy system to set up your blog in just a few clicks. YouTube has a few free tutorials for it.

Another option is to purchase a premium Wordpress template to make your site your own. If you install your Wordpress blog and want a shopping cart to go with it, then simply go to ECWID.com to set up a free shopping cart there. Then install the ECWID widget onto your Wordpress site.

Confused? YouTube can help with this, or, once again, you can hire someone on Elance.com or Guru.com to do this for you. I would title this project: "Install Wordpress with ECWID Widget + Template onto Bluehost." That again will take under 30 minutes for someone to do.

If there are any fun widgets you want added, include that in your project description as well. Even if you have a dozen widgets to add, it will take under an hour to install everything for you and should cost less than $200 for a professional programmer to get everything set up.

If you're confused by all my Web-speak, don't despair. You don't need to understand everything; just know how to hire someone who does. All of these programs we're mentioning were designed for people who are only tech savvy enough to check their email. If you can check and send an email, then you can work these programs.

If you don't want to deal with your own website at all, then I suggest using Etsy.

In fact, I usually suggest that moms wanting to start a business start with Etsy, then get a website up when they can. Etsy is great because it can bring in the much needed traffic at the beginning stages of a business.

When you're developing products, dealing with suppliers, configuring packaging and calculating pricing, bringing customers in the front door can be the last logistic you want to think about.

Etsy isn't foolproof for bringing in traffic though. You need to know how to optimize your listings. Then your listings will get all the free traffic you want and your Etsy shop can even get to the top of Google for even more traffic and sales.

Optimizing your Website and Etsy shop is easy, but takes a little time and I can write an entire book on that alone. This book is to get you set up. If, after you're set up, you're ready to start optimizing for more free traffic, go to my blog and I can help you with that too (http://richmombusiness.com).

Here are a few more shopping carts in case OsCommerce, Wordpress and Etsy don't fit your fancy.

Shopify—if you want to start an online store without the headache of your own website, then this is good solution. This is also a viable option if you want your store to be autonomous from other shops. This way, you don't have the competition in the same section of your site, like with Etsy. Shopify is continuously getting recognition, being a host to more than 25,000 online retailers including Pixar, Evernote, Epic Meal Time, and General Electric. Shopify hosts your shop on their site, so you don't ever have to worry about website or server issues. It costs money each month and has varied pricing plans. Shopify can be expensive, though, so if you can manage to install or hire someone to install OsCommerce I would suggest that over Shopify.

ECWID—I personally use and love this shopping cart because it works like a cloud shopping cart and it's also free. You enter your products once on ECWID.com, then add the ECWID widget to any blog, website or even right inside your Facebook fan page. The same products that you've entered at ECWID.com will show up everywhere that you've installed the widget. If you change a product on ECWID.com, it changes it on all of your widgets, even if you have a thousand of them on a thousand different sites. ECWID can be customized to match your branding with your HEX codes as well. They host and maintain your cart.

Amazon—tagged as the largest online retailer in the world, Amazon.com is a great place to start selling any of your real and virtual products, thanks to its continuously growing popularity and massive follower and customer base. Like Etsy, Amazon can bring in the traffic for you if you optimize your listings for people to find you.

BigCommerce—if you're looking not only for a shopping cart but also a business partner for web development and affiliate marketing business, then you might consider this option. I've personally never tried it, but I've heard a few people use it.

eBay—eBay is the largest and most popular auction site and is also a place where you can sell items in your own eBay shop. While Etsy is considered to be a boutique marketplace, eBay is considered to be a garage sale marketplace. It's harder to sell your items at a premium price on eBay and those who stop selling there claim that eBay's seller fees are simply too high, which is actually why I myself stopped selling there a while back. You can still get a lot of traffic on eBay though if you're willing to sacrifice a few pennies for the eBay fees.

SUMMARY

Choose your shopping cart system wisely. If you can, set up both an Etsy shop to bring in traffic and a website so your loyal customers can buy there without you having to pay extra Etsy fees.

16 | Reviews

Advertising is legalized lying.
—H.G. WELLS

Having good and legitimate reviews and testimonials for your company is crucial and can be more powerful than all the advertising dollars you can procure.

Now, more than ever, many big companies have fallen just because of a few bad reviews. Google "united airlines guitar video" for a good example of this.

One bad tweet or Facebook post on your page can ultimately end your company or put it in a horrible place where you are focusing on damage control instead of expanding, growing and loving every minute of it.

Companies are now hiring full-time employees just to monitor and build their reviews on social networking structures.

It's crucial to get some good reviews early on in your business. This will encourage first-time customers to trust you and order quickly, especially if you're on Etsy.

Some women I talk to feel that it's mean or too aggressive to ask for reviews. This is ridiculous. If I love someone's product and they ask for my review, I feel honored and want to help them get more business. Most people feel the same way.

Amazon, eBay and most big companies have automated review

emails sent out a few weeks after you place your order. This should be a standard feature in your own business too, even if it's not automated.

You don't have to be demanding and it's not rude to ask for a review (despite what others have said).

I usually email something like "I hope you really liked my ___. I worked on it personally for you. I would appreciate a review for the purchase if you have an extra second. Thanks in advance."

Keep it pithy, don't apologize for asking for the review, and always add "thanks in advance" as if they've already accepted. This isn't rude and they can always ignore your email if they don't have the time.

Sometimes people plan on giving good reviews, but they get busy and just plum forget. Send them a polite reminder once or twice. I wouldn't push it further than that, but it's ok to send them a reminder a couple times and some of them might even appreciate it.

Don't expect all of your reviews to be sparkling. I get suspicious myself when someone has all 5-star reviews for something and some of the reviews sound like ad copy. I'm sure you feel the same way.

One of my own most powerful reviews was from a customer that received an error in her order. She gave me 4 stars instead of 5 because of the error, but continued to say in the review that we fixed the mistake quickly and rushed a replacement order to her.

This review was more powerful than all my glowing reviews because it demonstrated that we listen to customers' complaints and fix any problems quickly that a customer might encounter.

Don't add your own reviews. People can smell this out. Don't do it. Encourage your customers to post reviews for you instead.

If you are scared of bad reviews—and you should be because it can ruin you—here are 5 of the best ways to avoid getting bad reviews.

1. Let customers know how you prefer to be contacted. I add a note into all of my packages saying "Please contact me via live chat immediately if there's something wrong with your order." This way, 99% of customers go to live chat first to catch me. They aren't fumbling around your site for phone numbers or email addresses. You can relieve a lot of that anxiety about a messed up order if you simply tell them right inside the shipment box how to contact you personally if something is wrong. This will stop them from posting their grievances in public.

2. Find ways to constantly collect feedback when customers receive their order. Once again, this goes back to asking for those reviews. You don't need to do it just to get glowing reviews and future orders; you need to do it to intercept anything that might have gone public if you hadn't contacted them in the first place. When you ask for a review, put in a disclosure that if there's anything wrong with your order you can be contacted directly at such and such email or phone number.

3. Avoid making the situation worse. Netflix is a good example of this. They wrote what may go down in history as the worst apology letter ever written. You can see their letter by googling "Netflix CEO Apology."

4. Develop a public relation policy if something goes wrong. If you mess up someone's order, have a strong policy in place and advertise it on your website as well. Write an apologetic letter with the policy in it before your angry customer reaches you. Then when they come, copy and paste it to them and offer to fix the mistake. It's vitally important that you figure out your apology letter before customers complain to you because this way, unwanted anger, denial and other emotions won't be added to the customer response.

5. Listen and respond quickly. Most angry customers just want
   to be heard and responded to quickly. Most importantly, they
   want to hear "I'm sorry." I took a law communications class in
   college and learned that 90% of lawsuits are actually dropped
   just because the people involved apologize to each other. Those
   two words can work wonders with angry customers. Apologize then fix the mistake. If customers are still angry—add
   free stuff. I have never met a person on this planet who doesn't
   love free stuff. Fix the mistake to the point where they are almost happy the mistake happened in the first place because
   now they get xyz free. Just make sure whatever free product
   you're sending is worth something so your customer doesn't
   roll their eyes and feel insulted on top of whatever problem
   they had in the first place.*

SUMMARY

Reviews are crucial to gain customer loyalty and trust. Contact customers after they receive their orders and before they contact you or
give reviews on your shop or social media. That way, if they have a
problem, you can fix it before they give a bad review.

---

* http://smallbiztrends.com/2011/09/15-ways-avoid-bad-online-reviews.html

17 Payment Options

Price is what you pay. Value is what you get.
—WARREN BUFFETT

If you are going to have a website besides just using Etsy, then you should really have a credit card processor and also a PayPal option if you can.

It's surprisingly easy to accept credit cards; you just need your business license and business bank account handy for the processing company and simply fill out the paperwork.

I have personally dealt with several credit card processing companies and they can be nightmarish and confusing.

In the end, I finally landed on authorize.net and have used them loyally ever since I signed on with them.

They have an easy to use back-end that you can sign into if you need to enter anyone's credit cards manually or you can refund partial or full credit card payments that way as well.

Even better is that a lot of those premade, turnkey, white-label scripts we've been talking about, like OsCommerce or ECWID, can be set up automatically to work with authorize.net so no extra coding or hiring programmers is required.

Authorize.net also has a wicked awesome-sauce support system and has never let me down when I've needed help.

PayPal is great, but you are limiting who your customers are, even though PayPal will accept credit cards without opening an account.

I personally love PayPal, but the logo with no other payment option can be polarizing and can make customers hesitate to make a purchase. If you want to be seen as a legitimate business, then you should sign up with authorize.net too and start taking credit cards.

If you sign up with another company to accept credit cards, like your bank, that's fab too. Just be aware that because you're running an online business, the logistics of the credit card processing company's software is vital and more important than the credit card processing rates.

Credit card processing companies will constantly be knocking down your doors trying to get you to switch your loyalties and they'll spout money and numbers to the ends of the earth.

Remember that in the case of an online business, it's more important that you use a system like Authorize.net that is universally used for all pre-coded online software to make your life easier. If you use your bank's credit card processing company, they'll tell you it's easy to program your cart to use their company, but it's a lie. It requires a lot of extra dollars to set it up and then another part of your cart might not work properly because of it.

I can't say it enough because I've fallen for many credit card processing companies who promise lower rates and better systems and have paid mucho dollars to programmers to try to integrate those systems into my shopping carts.

Authorize.net is also widely known for their security and you can even set up your shopping cart so you don't store a single credit card number. This is an amazing relief where liability is concerned.

Even if a hacker gets into your website, they won't be able to see anyone's credit card numbers. Let that burden be on Authorize.net and they take that burden extremely seriously.

SUMMARY

You need to take credit cards on your website in addition to PayPal to maximize your checkout procedures. Authorize.net is the best option for this and can connect with 95% of premade online software.

18 Shipping Options—Or who can ship for you

Whether you think you can or whether you think you can't,
you're right!
—Henry Ford

Let's discuss the difference between drop shipping, blind shipping and you shipping. Then we'll move onto shipping equipment and packaging if you decide to ship yourself.

Drop shipping is the most wonderful way to ship in the business world and it works like this:

Someone places an order with you and you then place an order with a wholesaler.

They ship out the order directly from their warehouse and put your name on it, as if it shipped from you.

Some companies will even keep your business cards and marketing materials on file to put inside the boxes.

Blind shipping is the second-most wonderful way to ship in the business world.

With blind shipping, you still place your order with the wholesaler and they ship your package for you, but the return address is the wholesalers' address and they simply leave off the name of the sender.

This way, customers don't see that it's coming from someone else and get confused.

Shipping yourself is ok too, as long as you are stocked up on shipping supplies and prepared to package your items correctly.

It's too easy to go cheap here but don't do it.

Your package needs to be neat, professional and even pretty if that's what your brand represents.

The way a customer feels while opening their package can determine if they will order again.

You can source inexpensive boxes from uline.com and I also personally use their "Kraft Paper Rolls" as a package filler.

With kids, packing peanuts or anything loose would be too messy and the rolls are easier to store and require less space. The Kraft paper rolls aren't pretty, but I don't want my filler to distract from the actual product.

You want your product to be the prettiest item in the box anyway.

Use a clear sleeve from clearbags.com to protect anything that might be made of paper or could get wet if the box is damaged.

You can also use tissue paper to wrap up your item and I personally use Uline's White Stretch Loops with some products because I don't want to spend a lot of time tying ribbons and bows.

As soon as the order is packaged, I write the order number on the box so I don't accidentally ship an order to the wrong customer.

Then I use the Weighmax 2822 scale to weigh the packages. You can get it on Amazon.com. It's small and can weigh letters up to 75 lbs.

Next, I go to USPS.com and log into my account. It's easy to sign up for an account and you just put your business credit or debit card on file to use each time and streamline things.

Now, simply place an order through click 'n' ship.

The first time you try this may be a little scary, but the process is simple. You just fill out a form with your customer's information. The shipping labels I use are also from Amazon.com from the seller 'printexx'.

I get 200 shipping labels for $8.55 and they're eligible for Amazon's free shipping if you combine it with something else and spend over $25.

These print like a dream through any home computer and they are compatible with USPS.com, so you don't have to do any adjusting. Just click 'n' print.

Simply hand your parcel to the local postman or you can even request the postman to come and pick up your package the next day, free.

You have the option to leave it on your porch or have him ring your door bell. I suggest having him ring your door bell the first time so you can speak to him. Tell him where you'll put the packages from then on and be sure it's in a place slightly hidden from the public view.

My postman and I know each other quite well and he knows the exact place to look for my packages on my porch to pick them up each time.

If you decide to drop your packages off at the post office, DO NOT stand in line. You already have your labels on your packages; they are ready to go. Just walk up to the front, (ignore the ugly stares you might get because they don't understand click 'n' ship), and put the package on the counter.

Say, "drop off!" Then walk out. Done.

This process is all very similar if you want to use UPS.com. However, they charge $4 to do pick-ups so I don't use them very often.

SUMMARY

Decide on a specific shipping option, whether it's drop shipping, blind shipping or shipping yourself. You can mix and match if needed as well. Learn click 'n' ship from USPS.com so you can have your packages picked up or drop them off without standing in line.

19 Basic HTML

You must either modify your dreams or magnify your skills.
—JIM ROHN

I hear it over and over again. Someone needs a line of wording changed on a website, but a programmer is taking weeks to make the changes or get back to that person.

I know the thought of learning website skills terrifies many folks getting started. But the truth is, you need to know at least the very basics so you aren't constantly hiring programmers just to change this wording or that wording or even just bolding a headline for you.

Having the skill of understanding HTML is invaluable and will save you a ton of money.

If you spend $25 on Lynda.com and treat learning HTML as a full-time job for one week, 8 hours a day, you'll pull your hair out and you might absolutely hate the process, but you'll never have to hire someone again to change out pictures or make the simple changes on your site.

Then you can use www.w3schools.com to look up any tag you might need after that. That site is free and after the week on Lynda.com you'll understand everything you see on w3schools.com.

If you ever get stuck, simply google your problem and you'll find even more customized free answers just for you.

You don't need to learn everything, but you do need to learn basics if you're going to get anywhere.

SUMMARY

I know it might be boring to you, but it's crucial to learn the basics of HTML. There really isn't an excuse not to learn it anymore now that there's Lynda.com, w3schools.com and YouTube.

20 Search Engine Optimization

*The entrepreneur always searches for change, responds to it, and
exploits it as an opportunity.*

—PETER F. DRUCKER

A search engine, such as Google, uses what we call spiders to case
the web, and then, in turn, when a user types in a key term into
Google, Google then uses that spider information to present what
Google thinks the user wants to the user.

Imagine a really extremely complicated algebra problem. This
algebra problem is kind of like an algorithm.

When Google first started out, they just sent the spider out with
an algorithm that said "ok, whoever has the search term most wins
and they get to the top of Google." Well, then the spammers came a
long and played Google. So Google had to change a little bit. And it
continued to be a game of cat and mouse until just recently Google
made some changes to stop spammers in their tracks.

I could write an entire book on SEO and, in fact, I have a whole
community built around it with video tutorials, books and over 75
tools, but for now, I want you to understand the basics. After you
get your business up and running you can hop on over to Rich-
MomBusiness.com and join the community to get your sites to the
top of Google.

This is also where you can learn how to optimize your Etsy listings to get to the top of Etsy because Etsy also has its own algorithms for their own website.

As you build your websites and shopping carts, though, I want you to understand some very basic SEO skills so you don't have to start from scratch when you want to start optimizing and perfecting your site later.

SEO stands for Search Engine Optimization. Imagine a delicious rhubarb pie with ice cream and whipped cream on top—you can imagine your own favorite pie if you like, rhubarb is my favorite.

Your site is that rhubarb pie. You want people to get to your site to enjoy the rhubarb pie.

Now imagine Google as the food critic. Google sends out agents (or food critics) all over the freeway and roads to find every single website in existence.

When Google reaches your site, will it like your site? Will it like your rhubarb pie? Will it even know that your site IS rhubarb pie?

This is why it's important to optimize your site. You have to optimize your site so Google loves it and wants to recommend it at the top of their search listings naturally.

The paid advertised listings aren't as trusted by consumers. The natural search listings are gold because those are the ones Google itself recommends. Those are also free.

Search Engine Optimization sounds so technical and scary, doesn't it? It can be quite simple, as long as you learn to have an SEO Mindset. Here are some basic SEO skills to learn while you're building your websites.

1. Your page title should have your first priority keywords. Your website has <title></title> tags inside the coding. Inside those tags are the most important words of your whole site. Google

thinks that the site must be about whatever you put in those title tags. Make sure your first priority key phrase is in that title. What do you want people to search on Google to find your site? That's what should be in that tag.

2. Your page title needs to also draw people into your site. Having your title tags utilizing your best keyword phrase is no longer enough. Google also keeps track of who clicks your site when they search that term. When someone reads your tag, but they are never clicking your site, Google takes this as a hint that your site might not have a lot of appeal, so Google ranks you lower. So your title must also draw people into the site.

3. Your description Meta tag. Meta tags are just a fancy code for robots to see and gather information from the raw code in your website. Your meta description tag usually looks something like this: <meta name="description" content="This is an example of a meta description. This will often show up in search results."> Your description tag should be a sentence that further draws customers into your site. Remember not to just write a list of keywords here or no one will click into your site and Google doesn't like this very much either.

4. Content. Flash sites are nice, but they usually rank incredibly low on Google. Why? They are extremely low on content. Google cannot read the wording in a flash file. You want Google to read the wording on your site and you want your wording to contain your keywords. Once again, do not stuff your site or Google can sense it and penalize you for it. Writing a nice long article for your front page helps and if you have a few links going into your site with more keywords that helps as well. Make sure your keywords are really close to the top and if you know html put your keywords in <h1></h1> tags or <b></b> tags as well.

5. Internal links. When you link to another page on your site, add your keywords to the anchor link. An anchor link usually looks like this: <a href="richmombusiness.com">KEYWORDS HERE</a>. Also, if possible, name the page .html file after your key terms too. Google loves when the name of your site is from your keywords too.

Remember, Google is like a food critic. You want them to be your biggest fan and try your rhubarb pie over and over again. So you need to put signs on the road over and over again that tell Google where to go for the yummy rhubarb pie.

Those road signs are the Search Engine Marketing of your SEO campaign. So where do you put up signs on the Internet? On other sites as back links. Google is changing its algorithms more and more to catch spam, so be extremely careful about building natural links and not spamming.

Now, more than ever, one good link on a well-known site will push you higher than a thousand links on a thousand lesser sites.

How do you get your link on other sites? Here are a few known options in the SEM world:

1. Reciprocal linking (i.e. you link to me and I'll link to you) used to be quite popular, but Google doesn't put any weight on that anymore.

2. Three way linking. Person A links to Person B then Person B links to Person C then Person C links back to Person A. There are sites you can sign up to for this and it helps to some extent, but make sure you aren't paying for the site links. Google hasn't seemed to penalize this way of linking, but their algorithms are becoming so smart that I'm sure Google will soon

give these links the same weight as reciprocal linking which is
little or nothing at all.

3. Back linking. This is Google's favorite type of linking. Basically, a higher page rank site links to yours and you don't link
back to theirs. This works wonders if the site linking to you
is high on Google itself or a .gov or .edu site. Google always
wants to list resources before sales pages and shopping cart
sites and having links on important sites shows Google that
your own site is a resource and you're not just trying to sell
something.

I highly suggest NOT paying for back linking. Do NOT subscribe or pay for link farms that promise you thousands of links in a
single day. These are not considered "white hat" methods and you
will be penalized by Google. The only way to get legitimate back
links is to do it manually and properly. You can pay to have an ad
and link on a high page rank site, or you can submit free content in
exchange for a back link on a blog or article site. If you don't want
to write for another blog and are simply selling products, you can
attempt to get a blogger to review your products and if they do,
most likely they'll add a nice juicy link back to your site right from
the blog post which is the type of authority link Google loves.

If you are on Etsy, you can still optimize your content, titles and
product descriptions. This not only will give you a better chance of
your products floating to the top of Etsy, but it will also show up
easier on Google right from your Etsy shop.

If you don't have the time to work on SEO/SEM then you can
outsource it, but be really careful. SEO specialists will make crazy
promises that they can't follow through on. I was burned myself on
this.

I was so lucky—I myself had worked up my Vegas invitation site to be in the top 5 search results on Google for the coveted search term "Las Vegas wedding invitations." I was getting orders constantly and loved every minute of it. Then I got greedy. I really wanted to be #1 on Google and thought an expert would be able to get me there.

After all, I only learned SEO for a few weeks and got myself to #5, so an expert should be able to get me to #1 right?

Someone contacted me and promised me that for $500/month, he could get me to that number one spot within a few months. What happened? The second I turned my site over, it completely dropped off the face of Google for that search term. I immediately lost orders. He said to be patient and wait for 3 months. I did ... that was my next mistake. I lost orders for 3 months while he continued to promise me day in and day out that he would be able to get me back up and even higher. He told me that Google has a delayed process and it would be up soon. (I later learned this was a lie.) Finally I let him go and had to take matters into my own hands. What a mistake.

I suggest learning the few SEO techniques you need to learn and do it yourself. Because you know your own business and your own clients, it will be better for you to do it yourself.

If, after you've learned a few basic SEO skills yourself, you want to hire out your SEO, that's perfectly fine. But you'll know quickly if they are making outrageous promises and can ask them straight up what they plan on doing with your site and you'll understand if those are good tactics or "black hat" tactics which can get you wiped off of Google completely.

SUMMARY

If you don't optimize your site, Google won't like or recommend it when it gets to your site. You know your industry better than any SEO specialist and that is more important than only knowing SEO. You should learn a few basic SEO skills, which only takes a few weeks, then you can hire it out if you need too.

21 Google Tools

To succeed in business, to reach the top, an individual must know all it is possible to know about that business.
—J. PAUL GETTY

Google has an enormous collection of tools. More businesses should take advantage of them. They seem so scary at first, but Google is a master at teaching as well, so you can learn everything they have to offer in just a day or two. Here are the most popular Google tools to use to drive more traffic, sales and or revenue to your sites.

1. Google Products

It is free to list your products here and every business should be doing it. All you need is an Excel spreadsheet of your products. Google itself even has the attributes and step-by-step instructions on how to submit your products.

2. Google Adwords

You pay Google to get your ads up and visible before people. You don't get the same return as learning SEO and getting naturally listed at the top of Google and you also have to pay to have those spaces. But it can return a nice result if done properly.

3. Google Adsense

Google pays you to put ads on your own website. When someone clicks your ads, you get paid. It's as simple as that. Google can even produce the ads in your own branded HEX code colors. You can choose text ads, small button graphics or even large banner ads. You have to weigh the pros and cons with this option. I started by having Adsense on my wedding invitation sites and promptly took them down because the ads were driving my own customers to my competitors' sites. If you have a blog or informational type site, then Adsense might be a better option for you than if you have just a shopping cart site.

4. Google Analytics

This is by far one of the best ways to learn about the traffic you are getting, where it's coming from and keywords that your website is being found for when people search Google. You simply copy and paste a code right into your website and voila. It's like magic. If you learn even the most basic of html skills, you should be able to do this yourself.

5. Google Authorship

Google Authorship is relatively new, but can help your website listings climb higher on Google and will also make them prettier. If you can claim your site with Google Authorship, then your photo and byline ("by Renae Christine" for example) get listed to your blog posts, website pages or products right on Google's search listings. It makes for a better click through rate as well and people trust those listings even more.

6. YouTube

Google now owns YouTube.com and they are constantly changing YouTube's layout and policies. They claim to have a master plan in mind for YouTube and clearly it's going to take a while for the YouTube algorithms and layout to be perfected the way Google wants it. But one policy has already been implemented and remains one of the easiest ways to get to the top of Google. If you make a video with your target keywords in the title and description of the video, then you have a higher chance of that video getting to the top of Google and the video will even have a video thumbnail next to it for a higher click thru conversion rate. Your YouTube video can demonstrate your products or you can simply do a sales video to get folks to go directly to your website.

You can double dip on YouTube if you claim Google Authorship on your YouTube channel. Then you can make a link for visitors to click right on your video to get to your website, so they don't even have to type in your website URL anymore.

If you're camera shy, then you can use TipCam or CamStudio to screen-capture your computer screen instead. You can screen-capture a Powerpoint presentation or tutorial or even show your website while you speak.

If you want to create an animated video, then go to GoAnimate. com or xtranormal.com.

If you want to make a montage video with photos and music, then go to stupeflix.com.

SUMMARY

Use Google's tools to drive in that extra bit of traffic or revenue. Get used to using Google's tools and when new ones come out be the first on board because it usually means your Google listings will get higher or look even better.

22 Social Media

The new source of power is not money in the hands of a few,
but information in the hands of many.
—JOHN NAISBITT

I've seen it too many times. Moms will grab a Facebook fan page or Twitter account and expect to generate sales instantly. I mean... you're getting free advertising, right? It should work, right?

Wrong.

Social Media is not Google. People go to social media to interact. It's like a cocktail party. People go to Google to solve a problem. They are going to Google in search of your product at the exact moment they are ready to buy.

Don't get me wrong, social media has a place in business too, but it's not to find new customers and it's not to sell to people.

Use Social Media as a reward for your loyal customers. Then sometimes you can gain new customers this way, but your ultimate goal for social media is to interact with your loyal customers by giving them discounts and inviting them to your cocktail party.

Remember that famous episode of The Office where Jim and Pam go to a dinner party at Michael and Jan's house? If you haven't seen this episode, it is a must so you can understand social media once and for all.

Michael inappropriately asks Jim to invest $10,000 in Jan's candle company, making for one of the most awkward moments of television history.

This is the exact feeling your friends, family and customers feel when you are asking them to buy your products on your social media fan pages.

Hallmark is a prime example of a fabulously run social media campaign. I encourage you to go to http://www.facebook.com/HALLMARK to see exactly how a social media campaign should be run. Most of their postings are quotes with photos or they feature their employees who create the cards or fun polls asking fans what their own opinion is on a recent holiday gift. If you're a fan of Hallmark, you don't want to be bombarded with "buy now" messages. You want to be invited to their cocktail party and not be sold to.

You can post discounts and deals and even recently sold products, but you should be engaging with your audience like they are your best friends. After all, you invited them to your cocktail party.

Kelly Paul from DirectlySuccessful.com has one of the very best programs I've ever seen that teaches exactly how to engage audiences properly with step-by-step tasks and tutorials. I've watched the students in her courses and their fan numbers always skyrocket and, in return, they end up getting sales and more fans.

One of the best ways to use social media is to get valuable suggestions and feedback from your customers. Ask them what flavor or color of product they want next. This is better than diamonds. Companies pay thousands, tens of thousands and even hundreds of thousands sometimes to poll their target market to get these answers. Now, all you need to do is ask on Facebook and Twitter and you'll know exactly what to make that your customers will buy.

Vicki Hyde Lewis is the master at this. She creates Flipzles for kids, which are double-sided puzzles that can be used as a puzzle and play set in one. She is smart to mass produce them so she can lower her prices for her customers, but it's vital that she gets the input from her customers on which design she should produce next.

Otherwise, she wastes a lot of money mass producing something that no one buys. For what it's worth, her Flipzles are the one item that my kids play with over and over again. Checkout her puzzles at http://www.facebook.com/Flipzles and tell her Renae sent you. I'm still trying to get her to make a glittery princess play set for my girls, but there aren't enough votes for that yet.

SUMMARY

Advertising and traditional marketing has gone the way of the unicorn. Use social media effectively by treating it like a cocktail party and not trying to sell to people. By providing rewards and interacting with your existing customers, you may be able to gain new customers as well. Social media can also be a valuable source of feedback from your customers.

23 Email Lists

The biggest regret I hear over and over again from business owners is that they didn't start an email list at the beginning of their business building.

Your email list is more important than any like on your Facebook page or any follow on Twitter.

When someone signs up on your email list, they are as loyal of a customer as it gets and you should be courting them as such.

Email them the very best discounts and even "unadvertised sales" that you don't allow the general public to see.

This makes your loyal customers even more loyal. They downright fall in love with you at this point.

Don't send lengthy emails. In fact, I hardly ever read an automated email if it's longer than a paragraph.

Get to the point and make it beautiful and branded.

My favorite program to achieve all of this is MailChimp.

It's not only free, it's the hippest emailing system on the planet. Their support and video tutorials also make me over the moon for them.

I created my own step-by-step tutorials on my YouTube channel just so you can set up your account on MailChimp, brand it with your logo and colors and even insert an email sign-up form on your website, Facebook and any other place that accepts html coding.

Why use MailChimp as opposed to a Gmail group list? The

laws state that users must have certain information on the emails you send them. You need to have your information plus a way for folks to unsubscribe if they don't want to receive further emails from you.

MailChimp adds all of this in your email automatically, and thus keeps track of all your subscribers and unsubscribers and will even send you emails when someone subscribes or unsubscribes to you.

I won't lie. It hurts when someone unsubscribes.

MailChimp can be used in a hundred different ways, but while you are just getting started, you just need to sign up and add a sign-up form on your website and Facebook page.

You can entice people further to sign up for your mailing list by offering them something free in return. Make sure what you offer is of value or you'll just have people rolling their eyes and losing respect for you and your company.

SUMMARY

Use a Mailing List system like MailChimp or aweber to keep track of your very best customers. Woo them with discounts, secret sales and free goodies if they spend a certain number of dollars. Start your mailing system when you start your business or you'll regret it later.

24 Bloggers, Vloggers, The Press

*Will a juicy press mention bring legions of new customers to
your business? Maybe. But, more often than not, it won't bring
you the flurry of new customers you expect.*

— MELISSA CASSERA[*]

Too often we're told that in order to get a ton of sales at once, your
product needs to be featured on a well-known blog or vlog. This
just isn't the case, unless it's Oprah's blog or vlog.

You should actually be using those reviews in a different way.
Instead of expecting instant sales from the blog post itself, use those
reviews and endorsements to get more sales yourself.

Use quotes from the review on your own website as a product
testimonial. Link to the review on your social media as bragging
rights. Offer a discount to those blog readers as extra incentive to
buy quickly.

When I review products, I tell the company or person that created those products that they can embed the video right onto their
website and use it how they like.

Have you ever visited a website and seen lots of logos from reputable companies like Forbes or Newsweek with a "featured in"

---

[*] http://www.ohmyhandmade.com/2013/what-we-know/media-coverage-cash-the-
surprising-things-you-need-to-know/

above it? Those links and logos are called authority bling and can bring you trustworthiness, customer loyalty and even extra sales.

So the product review might not have brought in sales over at Forbes.com, but it will bring you more sales by having the Forbes logo on your own website.

I've even seen some Etsy shop owners type out what I've said about their products in my vlog right inside their Etsy product pages in quotes and with a "~Renae Christine from Rich Mom Business" next to it, showing that a 3rd party loves those products.

Understand that the power of a 3rd party promoter who isn't an affiliate of your products is more powerful than the promotional blog post itself.

Even if that blog post brings in a thousand sales in a day, you would still be doing a disservice to yourself by not adding the testimonial to your site permanently to stand as 3rd party authority bling to last five years down the road and get even more sales.

Because you might not get a hundred sales as soon as a 3rd party blogger hits "publish" does that mean you shouldn't send your products their way? No.

You need testimonials from customers and the media as well, and there's no other way of getting testimonials from the media. You simply have to mail something off to them in a pretty package and hope they review it.

A few tips to enhance the chances of getting your products reviewed by the media include:

Address the blogger, journalist or press person by their correct first name. You'd be surprised at how often someone calls me Christine and it makes me wonder if they've ever seen a single one of my videos. I even sign all of my blog posts and social media posts with "XOXO Renae", so why would they call me Christine?

Mention something specific to their blog that shows you are a constant visitor. Don't pretend to be a constant visitor unless you are. If you're not a constant visitor, then subscribe to their email lists and wait for a month, constantly visiting, before you send on products.

Comment on their blog posts and contribute to the overall conversation. Then when you send products to that person, they will recognize your name and be more inclined to review your products.

Send a "thank you in advance" card with the products assuming that they'll do the review. Don't be forceful, but a thoughtful thank you card can go a long way. For me, if the thank you card is on a piece of letterpress, it's guaranteed to get my attention.

Use wording that you've seen the blogger or journalist use. Whenever I see the words "awesome-sauce," "crazi-sauce" or "besties" in a card accompanying a product, I know that that person is one of my besties and it makes me want to review their products before I've even opened the box.

Mention a recent blog post or article that blogger has written. This also shows that you're paying attention and that's all bloggers and journalists really want.

Don't go cheap. If someone did all of the above and I looked in the box to find a cheap 10 cent bookmark printed off their home computer advertising their ebook, I would throw it away instantly. I actually had someone contact me, asking me to review her products, and when I gave this girl my address, she refused to send me the products to review. This girl told me she would only send me products to review if I hosted a party for her multi-level marketing company. Bloggers and vloggers are doing you a favor by giving you an unbiased 3rd party unaffiliated review and if you start by insulting them, then they are less inclined to speak to you in the future for pretty much anything.

Melissa Cassera has an amazing program at http://www.make-headlines.com to help you perfect the skill of getting the press to notice you without taking a lot of your time doing it.

SUMMARY

Send your products to various bloggers, vloggers and press members to review. Catch their attention by knowing their blog or previously written articles. Don't expect sales to come flowing in when the product review goes live. Instead, use it for testimonials, bragging rights and authority bling for your sites and product pages.

25 Employees, Freelancers, Contractors

Management is nothing more than motivating other people.

— LEE IACOCCA

An independent contractor—also sometimes called a freelancer, is considered self-employed. They have their own business and their business is usually themselves and they hire themselves and their services out to you and your company. They deal with their own taxes and you send them a 1099 at the end of the year. You can hire as many independent contractors or freelancers as you like.

An employee is someone who is employed by your company. Employees submit a W-9 form and you take out taxes and are responsible for paying their taxes for them frequently. You can't always have employees when you have a sole proprietorship formation of a company.

Which should you use for your company? The IRS doesn't even really know. The following is a direct excerpt from irs.gov:

> *"There is no 'magic' or set number of factors that 'makes' the worker an employee or an independent contractor, and no one factor stands alone in making this determination. Also, factors which are relevant in one situation may not be relevant in another."**

---

* http://www.irs.gov/businesses/small/article/0,,id=99921,00.html/

Tim Ferris, author of *The 4-Hour Work Week*, became a multi-millionaire before the age of 33. But in his book, he touts that if you ask him how many employees he has, he'll tell you his company only has himself as an employee.*

How does he accomplish this? He hires contractors and free-lancers.

As a stay-at-home mom business, this might be your best option as well.

This can save a lot of headaches and legalities when it comes to taxes, hiring and even firing. You don't have to worry as much about a lawsuit if you let a contractor go. You have to worry a lot more about lawsuits when firing an employee.

My biggest regret was delaying in contracting out tasks after I had enough money to pay someone to do them.

I was pregnant and on bed rest for two back-to-back pregnancies and yet I continued to run my body into the ground through my business. When I had my babies, I took exactly 24 hours off, then it was back to work.

I kick myself for doing that. If I had only known that there was a way to pay assistants to help. I could have enjoyed my babies as infants instead of attempting to nurse while working at my computer.

You do not have to pay a lot for help and you can't expand your business without it.

If your business is at home and can be worked on at various times of the day, high school and college students can become the most amazing assistants ever.

One of my all-time favorite assistants was a student at a local college. She appreciated being able to keep her own hours. She changed them on a weekly basis and even changed them each se-

---

* Source: http://globalinternetsuccess.com/tag/multi-millionaire

mester as her classes changed. She appreciated the flexibility when important tests and events came up and thus needed a day off.

In turn, she pays attention to scrupulous details and even does extra tasks I ask, like mailing out extra packages. If any of you saw the contest I ran on my YouTube channel where I painted my hand with peanut butter and spread it all over a sheet of copy paper, it would make you happy to know that my assistant mailed out the winner's peanut butter hand as soon as she came in . . . after she stopped laughing.

My only disagreement with Tim Ferris's book is that he says to hire assistants from India. I went through 5 assistants and had to fire each one because of either a language barrier or they were extremely rude and condescending when they found out I was a woman, something Tim Ferris never had to deal with so he couldn't warn me about it in his book.

I nearly gave up when I listened to a one hour webinar hosted by Brad Callen explaining that outsourced work like that should be given to Filipinos. They grow up learning English and have an Americanized culture. It wasn't mentioned in the webinar, but in hiring Filipinos, I've found they have a much better respect for women bosses too.

You can also look to local internship programs to find good help and that can be the least expensive of all.

You really shouldn't be hiring anyone though, until your own business is up and running and you have a system going.

The only reason I'm mentioning it now is so that after your business gets set up and roaring and down the road you start to feel like you're running on a treadmill and about to quit, recognize that hiring assistants is an option no matter what your business is and I can help you with that when the times comes as well.

SUMMARY

Create a business system and even a training system before hiring an assistant. Don't hire from India; if you must outsource, outsource to the Philippines, especially if you're a woman.

The Formula Laid Out Step by Step

When you're a carpenter making a beautiful chest of drawers,
you're not going to use a piece of plywood on the back,
even though it faces the wall and nobody will ever see it.
You'll know it's there, so you're going to use a beautiful piece of
wood on the back. For you to sleep well at night, the aesthetic,
the quality, has to be carried all the way through.
—STEVE JOBS

Right about now, you might feel overwhelmed at the long to-do list ahead of you. There are so many aspects to running a business that when you're starting the road it can be easy to see all the hard work needed and quit before you begin.

I feel the same way before I start each new business myself and I don't pretend that this is a short checklist that you can finish in ten days or less like many books pretend to advertise, "10 steps to starting a business in 10 days!"

No. It doesn't work that way. Those books aren't funny and are out to make a quick buck.

I understand that the list below is long, but it is better to have a looong to-do list to check off than having to go back before online businesses were proven to be successful. Online businesses back then were only successful for the big boys. I personally fell through all the cracks, made all the mistakes and learned what works. You won't have to do any of that. Now, more than ever, there is a level playing field with those big companies. You will be able to get to where I am in half the time it took me—even with this long checklist.

Keep in mind that this is a physical book and while it will be updated every few years, it has the limitation of not having instant and important breaking news that can make your business skyrocket. So follow my blog at http://www.richmombusiness.com and become a community member there, and you will have the most amazing edge against even the biggest companies, especially in the community where everyone is a news breaker and not just myself.

Idea & Research

1. Look up your idea and possible search terms at http://tools.seobook.com/keyword-tools/seobook/.
2. Research your competition on Google. How bad is it? Do all the websites have your type of product linked directly from the search or are the links redirected to similar items but not the same thing. Also check competitors on Etsy and see if folks are buying the actual products you intend to sell.
3. How can you make the product better than your competition?
4. Write a one to two sentence elevator pitch that will both explain and sell your product.

Product Creation & Testing

5. Create your product.
6. Test your product.

7. Recreate your product.

8. Retest your product.

9. Repeat steps 5 - 8 until someone says they can't live without your product. If this takes a while, do some research into why the public doesn't love your product as much as you love it. Ask strangers to test your product and ask for their honest opinions and what they would improve about your product. This can be the hardest part of starting a stay-at-home business sometimes, but it will be well worth it when you have one dynamite product that folks can't live without. No amount of marketing can save a horrible product. When someone does say they love your products, ask if you can quote them on your websites. This can be very valuable.

Brand

10. Decide on the name of your main company. Pick a name that can be an umbrella for multiple businesses spread across multiple industries.

11. Search Trademarkia.com to see if your company's name has been trademarked. There's nothing worse than starting a company, paying for designers, websites and more, then being told you have to start over because someone owns the copyright to that name. I've never experienced it, but I've heard many horror stories.

12. Hire a logo designer or grab a premade logo from Kelly J. Sorenson's Etsy Shop. Do NOT use a logo generator or funny online software to do this for you.

13. Be sure to ask for the hex color codes from your designer so you can brand everything you create for your company.

Legalities, Finance & Security

14. Sign up for your business licenses.
15. Create your business plan.
16. Sign up for your resale tax certificate if needed.
17. Sign up for your DBA or Fictitious Firm Name if needed.
18. Sign up for any additional licenses or insurance that may be required for your product.
19. Research any further contracts or legalities you may need in order to cover your businesses liabilities.
20. Sign up for a PayPal account and Authorize.net so you can accept payments.
21. Decide if you're going to play accountant or hire one to track your finances, losses and gains.
22. Figure out a basic system for pricing items and crunching the numbers when an item sales.
23. Secure a back-up system of some kind if your main work is on your computer and can be ruined by a single computer crash.

Investing

24. Purchase or make enough of your first product for about 20 orders. If this is too much of an investment or your product is an expensive item, then prep less. If your item needs to be made fresh, make sure you have on hand the ingredients that won't go bad.
25. Purchase your packaging supplies. Pretty items are nice, but branded packaging is even better and can end up the same price if you purchase in bulk.
26. Purchase business cards, inserts and stickers to put on your packaging. Make sure your website and preferred method of

contact are on every one of them in case there's a problem with someone's order or they just want to re-order.

27. Create your initial products and photograph them or hire someone to photograph them.

Set-Up

28. Sign up for Etsy and/or create your own shopping cart or blog website to coincide.
29. Brand Etsy. Brand your website.
30. Add your website to your email signature.
31. Optimize your website, products, social sites, Etsy shop and Etsy listings.
32. Sign up for a free MailChimp account and create a new list for your customers who want to stay informed of your sales and discounts.

Html + Seo

33. Learn the basic HTML tags <a href"">></a>, <b></b>, <h1></h1>, <img src=""></>, <p></p>
.
34. Research a few keywords that you want to be found for, then enter those in your website meta tags and product titles and descriptions.

Social Media & Media

35. Sign up for a Facebook Fan page, Twitter, G+ and Pinterest account.
36. Brand your social media sites.

37. Send your products to your favorite bloggers with a "thank you in advance note" in hopes that they'll review your products. Add those fabulous review quotes to your site, shops and social media too.

Extra Help

38. Hire accountants, contracted freelance employees, assistants and any other consultants or helpers that you might need to keep your business going without a hitch.

Going Live

39. List your products on Etsy and your Facebook page.
40. Post an announcement on your social media sites that you are having a grand opening; invite others to like your page.
41. Post a grand opening discount on all your social media and add a branded coupon with the discount code if possible.

Expanding

42. Ask those who purchased your products to write a review in your Etsy shop.
43. Start engaging your fans on your social media. Ask them what product they want to see come out next.
44. Find unique ways to produce customer loyalty like "Fan of the Week" giveaways on your social media or find blogs that also feature giveaways.
45. Continue to optimize and learn SEO as you go so your business can slowly get bigger and gain more traffic.

46. Email sales and discount messages exclusively to those on your MailChimp list. Make sure they understand that it's a "secret sale" or "unadvertised sale" so they feel special.

Support

47. Whatever you do, don't quit. Get as far as you can, then get the support you need at RichMomBusiness.com. If you can't sign up for the paid community, subscribe free to get 2-minute, funny, daily YouTube videos that will help you slowly grow your business inch by inch.
    - http://www.facebook.com/byrenaechristine
    - http://twitter.com/byrenae
    - http://instagram/renaechristine
    - http://pinterest.com/renaechristine
    - http://www.youtube.com/RichMomBusiness

27 Fun tools that make running your business deliriously fun

A business has to be involving, it has to be fun, and it has to exercise your creative instincts.

—Richard Branson

Let's face it, if you haven't started a business and you've gotten to this point, you are probably overwhelmed. Remember that a business can take as long as a year just to set everything up.

Don't despair though. Running a business can be downright addicting with some of these fabulous tools.

http://tweetreach.com—*How far did your tweet travel?*

http://timehop.com—*What were you doing a year ago?*

http://www.getsocialscope.com—*A mobile inbox for your social networks.*

http://nutshellmail.com—*Manage social networks with email.*

http://www.virtualchrome.com—*Run a full desktop version web browser on your iPad.*

http://indiemade.com—*Another website option.*

http://amplicate.com—*Find out what people love and hate on social media.*

http://www.addshoppers.com—*Social analytics and sharing apps built for retailers.*

http://www.howsociable.com—*Measure your brand.*

http://northsocial.com—*Facebook app buffet at the click of a button.*

http://www.brandmymail.com—*Brand your Gmail emails to look professional.*

http://www.socialmention.com—*Like Google alerts, but for social media.*

http://www.tabjuice.com—*Turn your Facebook into a boutique.*

http://bit.ly—*Shorten your URLs. Free for Twitter and Facebook.*

http://crowdspoke.com—*Get high quality content delivered to you for social media.*

https://www.postling.com—*Social media management tools.*

http://tellafriend.socialtwist.com—*Acquire new customers through social referral marketing.*

http://hootsuite.com—*Social media dashboard.*

http://marketing.grader.com/—*HubSpot's Marketing Grader grades your marketing.*

http://wordpress.org/extend/plugins/scribe/—*Scribe SEO Plug-in for Wordpress.*

http://wordpress.org/extend/plugins/wp125/—*WP125 Plug-in, advertising plug-in for Wordpress.*

http://www.bluehost.com—*The best hosting company out there for startups and one of the cheapest too.*

http://trello.com—*Organize with virtual sticky notes on a virtual bulletin board. Keep it private or add members and contractors.*

http://www.responsinator.com—*See how your website looks on every mobile device and tablet. (I use this all the time.)*

http://getpocket.com—*The stuff you discover online, ready when you are.*

http://ecwid.com/—*A free cloud shopping cart for Facebook, Wordpress and more.*

http://chirp.io—*A new app that helps share files easily on the go. It literally sings info. from one iPhone to another.*

http://www.vappapp.com/—*Trigger your iPhone camera with any sound.*

http://evernote.com/skitch/—*The Skitch app gets your point across with fewer words by using annotations, shapes and sketches.*

https://www.mywickr.com—*Self-destructing text messages.*

https://catch.com/—*Touch the capture wheel with your thumb to capture ideas and inspirations with text, photos, checklists and voice memos.*

SUMMARY

Check out all of these awesome tools, apps and programs. Then don't forget to subscribe to my daily blog to find even more apps and fun software programs on a daily basis. http://richmombusiness.com

Extra goodies

My favorite blogs, websites, books and resources: Don't forget to tell them Renae Christine sent you. Then they'll treat you real nice.

http://www.theperfectpalette.com—*Amazing examples of color palettes. Great branding tool.*

http://iheartorganizing.blogspot.com—*Organization in pretty ways.*

http://theinvitationblog.com—*A fabulous stationery blog.*

http://goodsie.com/store/lifenreflection/—*Premade party kits, cards, scrapbook kits and more.*

http://www.etsy.com/shop/sararubendall—*Sarah Rubendall premade Etsy branding kits.*

http://www.etsy.com/shop/hellogorgeousbath—*Amazing soaps branded with vintage flair.*

http://www.etsy.com/shop/MickeysCreations—*The best custom made bags ever.*

http://kellyjsorenson.etsy.com/—*Premade graphics, logos, and branding kits.*

http://addictivecosmetics.etsy.com/—*Handmade gorgeous makeup.*

http://www.etsy.com/shop/FiddledeeDeeCraft—*Felt foods for your kids' play sets. My kids love these.*

http://missblondiexoxo.blogspot.com/—*A little bit of this and that.*

http://www.freewardchoirmusic.com—*Free, beautiful arrangements of religious hymns.*

http://www.etsy.com/shop/MyraMelinda—*Vintage Etsy shop.*

http://www.etsy.com/shop/destemps—*Dessert-wear.*

http://www.etsy.com/shop/irisandlily—*Boutique tech cases.*

http://www.etsy.com/shop/bettula—*Hand-crafted birch bark jewelry and home decor.*

http://www.etsy.com/shop/shineinvitations—*Swoon worthy wedding stationery.*

http://www.etsy.com/shop/BradensGrace—*Chalkboard labels and stands.*

http://www.etsy.com/shop/michaelswoodworks—*Personalized Carved Custom wood signs.*

http://www.etsy.com/shop/uncommon—*Homey meets modern feel for home decor.*

http://www.etsy.com/shop/YourGuiltyPleasure—*Handmade dessert jewelry.*

http://www.etsy.com/shop/AidenModernVintage—*My favorite earrings.*

http://sharedjoy.etsy.com—*Fabulous headbands.*

http://www.eddieandeva.com—*Delicious, organic soaps.*

http://www.knittykitty.com—*Amazingly comfy yet sexy knitimates.*

http://www.youtube.com/thetomcoteshow—*The Tom Cote Show.*

http://www.elance.com—*My go-to for freelancers. Make sure you check reviews and interview them before projects start, so you know if they understand English well.*

http://www.guru.com—*My 2nd go-to for freelancers. Make sure you check reviews and interview them before projects start so you know if they understand English well.*

https://www.elance.com/s/joomexp/—*My personal website program-*

mer. Also an SEO/SEM expert. Just don't overload him to the point that he can't do my own jobs.

https://www.elance.com/s/amsoftech/—*Another fantastic programmer and SEO expert. Understands English really well.*

https://www.elance.com/s/paralegalpros/—*Legal research and writing expert. Responds quickly.*

https://www.elance.com/s/magilldaniel—*Article writing, editing, copywriting, website copy. He has a dreamy British accent to boot.*

https://www.elance.com/s/coffee2go/ - Martin Coffee—*Offers a host of communications solutions including editing, copywriting, copyediting and proofreading.*

Business Reads

Problogger | http://amzn.to/UIMVGw

Emyth Revisited - Why Most Small Businesses Fail and What to do About it | http://amzn.to/UHL36w

Platform - Get Noticed in a Noisy World | http://amzn.to/YxYZ0b

Advertising Headlines That Make You Rich | http://amzn.to/WUxETN

Words that Sell: More than 6000 Entries to Help You Promote Your Products, Services, and Ideas | http://amzn.to/XYumy9

Etsy-preneurship | http://amzn.to/YImnrY

Marketing with Video Using Secret Keyword Tactics | http://amzn.to/Yeqxpb

The 4-Hour Workweek, Expanded | http://amzn.to/TRYi2W

Who Moved My Cheese? | http://amzn.to/UHO2M9

Best Practices for Persuasive Presentations | http://amzn.to/WUACYh

Free Youtube Tutorials

Installing OsCommerce onto Bluehost: http://www.youtube.com/watch?v=FEipuxTeGhA

Setting up a MailChimp account and campaign: http://www.youtube.com/watch?v=pzCIl77h3Fc

Using ECWID and installing it to Facebook: http://www.youtube.com/watch?v=R_bKy6pliZ0

Support

Don't try to build your business alone. It can become extremely stressful and if you don't have like-minded work-at-home moms to help you de-stress, you'll completely break down. I still have a horrible break down crying video on my own YouTube channel to prove it.

My forum is an awesome place to start and there isn't any spam or scams going on in there. It's all love and support.

Here are some other blogs that can help keep you motivated as well.

http://www.ramblingsofawahm.com

http://www.mompreneurmogul.com

http://www.mominvented.com

http://www.enlistmoms.com

http://www.moneymakingmommy.com

http://www.mommamaven.com

http://www.marieforleo.com

http://www.mama-press.com

http://www.seedmommy.com

http://www.momventures.com

http://www.womenonthefence.com

http://www.mombizcoach.com

http://www.ohmyhandmade.com

http://worksmartmompreneurs.com

http://www.milliondollarmompreneur.com

http://www.businessamongmoms.com

http://www.somewhatsimple.com

http://www.mommybreadwinner.com

http://www.specialmompreneurs.com

http://www.momentrepreneurcenter.com

http://www.inspiredworkingmoms.com

http://www.wordofmomradio.com

http://www.daintymom.com

http://www.thechristianmompreneur.com

http://thesitsgirls.com

http://www.momincorporated.com

http://www.mompreneurwellness.com

http://www.momgetsalife.com

http://www.ragstostitchesblog.com

http://www.smartmompreneur.com

http://www.workingmother.com

http://www.launchgrowjoy.com

http://www.marketingcreativity.com

http://www.mothersanddaughtersinbusiness.com

http://www.themompreneur.com

http://www.escapefromcubiclenation.com

http://www.paysoncooper.com

http://thebusinessofbeingamom.com

http://www.foundingmoms.com

http://www.glamalife.com

http://www.lulyb.com

http://www.girlreimagined.com

http://www.themomiverse.com

http://www.internetbasedmoms.com

http://www.theworkathomewoman.com

http://www.supermomentrepreneur.com

http://www.itsawahmlife.com

http://theworkathomewife.com

http://www.mompreneursteps.wordpress.com

http://MelanieKisell.com/blog

http://MompreneursOnline.com

http://www.handmadeology.com

About Renae Christine

One sunny afternoon, many years ago, an 8-year-old girl set up a lemonade stand on the side of the road. Of course it wasn't selling actual lemonade. No, this girl simply crumpled up bits of old newspaper and put them inside plastic snack bags. She labeled each bag 'GARBEG' [meaning garbage] in big, black permanent marker.

When folks drove by, they were so intrigued by what this little girl was selling that they had to stop and ask.

"My mom says everyone buys garbage, so I'm selling garbage."

That girl came home with more money that day than probably any other kid in the history of lemonade stands. And not a drop of lemonade had been expended!

So entertained were the people who stopped to find out what this girl was doing, they simply had to buy a bag of garbage and take it home to show their spouses.

Renae was that little girl and that was the start of her entrepreneurial career.

CPSIA information can be obtained
at www.ICGtesting.com
Printed in the USA
BVHW071001280119
538455BV00037B/193/P